To my wife Liz,
For being my sounding board and
for your endless support and unconditional love.
Thank you for giving me wings to fly.

EMPIRE PUBLICATIONS
1 Newton St., Manchester M1 1HW
© Joe Matera 2024

LOUDER
THAN WORDS

BEYOND THE BACKSTAGE PASS

JOE MATERA

EMPIRE
PUBLICATIONS

Louder Than Words:
Beyond The Backstage Pass

Joe Matera

Contents

Foreword

J oe Matera is a rock music fan, perhaps like no other… because he writes about what he's passionate about. My co-writer, Jim Vallance, knows Joe the same way I do. In that he has followed and documented what we've done over the years and shown some genuine enthusiasm for rock music generally.

I think you'll find Joe's book fascinating and you'll undoubtedly find out new things about some of the music you love.

Bryan Adams

Introduction

It was 2021, just as some semblance of post-pandemic normality was resuming, when I was first contacted by Joe Matera with a request for a YouTube interview. I learned that Joe is himself a touring musician and genuine rock music aficionado with many European tours under his belt, as well as a whole host of musical publications and interviews. The subject matter of our online conversation was to be the 1980s song I'd sung and written, 'Everybody's Got to Learn Sometime' and the Korgis album from which it emanated, *Dumb Waiters.*

My long-time musical mates and I had recently resurrected The Korgis a few years prior and had just released an album of brand-new tunes entitled *Kartoon World,* so any opportunity to commune with the general public was most welcome. Not only that, I was intrigued by the Antipodean connection: Joe is a native of Victoria, Australia and was calling from there and my writing and performing partner in the 21st century Korgis band, Al Steele, is also an Aussie and knows Joe's area very well.

So that's the background, but here's the thing: I was delighted by Joe's detailed research and obvious passion for the 1980s (not to mention the 70s, 90s and noughties) and as I quickly began to discover, his enduring fascination and love for an incredibly diverse range of musical styles and genres.

And this is what you will find when you delve into this wonderful rock music compendium. Want to savour some touring stories from Snowy White playing with Pink Floyd? A heartfelt and comprehensive appreciation of the late Gerry Rafferty? The full untold story of what really caused the unravelling of American rocker Billy Squier's career? Or how about the revealing chapter on the bands that were hyped to be the next big thing but which ended up going nowhere:

remember doubleDrive, Hoggboy or Phantom Planet?

And there's Joe's recent on-the-road adventure with Canned Heat and The Animals — analysis, appreciation and abundant anecdotes in one volume?

It's all here!

James Warren
The Korgis

Preface

The artists featured and music discussed in this book have influenced my own life and music. All have, at some point, intersected with my own musical journey. Some I have been fortunate enough to have worked with, some I have gone on tour with and played shows as their support act, while others I've interviewed and spent time with in either hotels, backstage areas and various other locations. And some, through the telling of *their* story, shed much light on the nuts and bolts on the workings of the music industry, as well as the qualities they inhabit, that shape their character and who they are both as human beings and as artists, which in turn informs their own music.

This book is an attempt to not only give an insight into what lies behind the curtain of the music industry, and dispel some of the myth making, but to also give a front row seat to what life on the road is like, to the alchemical process of making music, both from an artist's perspective and as merely an observer and music fan. In the process giving a little more substance to, and understanding of, life lived in the musical sphere.

In an interview I conducted with guitarist Paul Dean from Canadian rock band Loverboy, Dean summed it up succinctly in stripping away that public persona when he stated: "Sometimes people see us together at an airport and ask if we're in a band. My usual response is, 'we're going to a plumber's convention'". Loverboy lead singer Mike Reno put it in a more accurate perspective when he said, "We're waiters; waiting for our plane to board, waiting in the lobby for our room to be cleaned, waiting for the runner, who's usually late, to take us to sound check. And the worst part, that last interminable ten minutes before the lights go down, and we finally get on stage."

1: I Can Hear Music

usic has always been part of my life. From the moment I was born I heard sounds that had a rhythm to them. They say one chooses a profession, but music chose me. It was like the pied piper played his tune and it awakened something in me. It's given me a life I would have never imagined that I would live and experience when I first heard those sounds.

Looking back there have been times where, deep down, I just knew what I was here for. One such moment occurred when I first picked up the guitar at the age of fifteen. I can still remember vividly that feeling, as I was playing away one night in my bedroom, this feeling came over me, I don't know how to describe it in words, but I just knew instantly at the moment that I would play the guitar for the rest of my life.

But going further back, music was what defined me, made me who I am, opened the door to a world that for me, as an only child, brought me company, friendship, and loyalty. It was my refuge from the outside world. In some of my darkest moments music has pulled me through, saved me, helped me understand, guided me and connected me to the deeper mysteries of life and the interconnectedness of human existence. It is food for my soul and spirit. Then, as I discovered my favourite music artists and lost myself in their music, it pulled me in even more, where now I wanted to know more about the artist: their music, their story, and what lay behind the music they created and performed.

A pivotal moment in my musical life came when I was ten years old. *Explosive Hits '75* was a compilation album put out by EMI Australia of some of the then current chart hits in Australia. This was part of a series that were issued throughout the 1970s and the hits featured were usually by the artists that were on the roster of the EMI record label. I first bought this record when it came out, and the artists featured here ranged from international acts such as Bay City Rollers, Pilot, Steve Harley and Cockney Rebel, The Glitter Band, Linda Ronstadt and Al Martino to Australian acts such as AC/DC and Sherbet. These albums were hugely popular with the record buying music fans, especially younger music fans such as myself.

These types of compilations were great as a lot of the time they would inspire you to delve further into a particular artist's catalogue as the albums usually came with an inner sleeve that featured information on the artists' latest album from which that hit single was taken.

This album holds a special place for me as it's pivotal to my music life story. Decades later I met and interviewed many of the artists on this album, I even ended up touring with a few of them and became friendly with them. Never in my wildest dreams as a ten-year-old would I have ever imagined this happening.

Nineteenth century German philosopher Friedrich Nietzsche wrote in his 1889 book *Twilight of the Idols* that, "without music, life would be a mistake". And in the early 19th century fellow German philosopher Arthur Schopenhauer also declared music to be the highest art form.

"Music is magical," affirms Marty Jourard, keyboardist and saxophonist from 1980s hit-makers, The Motels. "You're making something out of nothing with music. It can affect people so immediately, and instantly just go right into you without you analysing it. The response to music is an unintellectual process". Touché.

I recall around the age of seven imagining myself being in a popular band that were releasing albums and performing for audiences around the world. I had an active imagination. And I used to daydream regularly. At night I would sit at the kitchen table, which was covered in a clear plastic tablecloth, the usual type of furniture setting found in an Italian family's household, and I started sketching these imaginary album covers. I came up with a fictional band name, The Flies, and began designing fictional album titles and covers for the band. For example I would have the title, *The Flies Fly By* as a title for their debut or *The Flies Live in Concert* as an album they would release three or four albums into their career. It was totally fictional but I loved losing myself in this world. It is interesting because even at such a young age I seemed to know the progress of a band's career trajectory. Yet it was all in my young imagination.

What was uncanny though was that years later I found out that there was an actual band called The Flies, an English psychedelic pop band that had a few minor hits in the sixties, one of which was their cover of "(I'm Not Your) Stepping Stone", made more famous by The Monkees. The only reason why I came up with the band name was because it was a similar insect name to The Beatles. I was totally unaware at the time of the real Flies nor had I ever heard of them. Decades later I would be doing the exact thing I had day-dreamed about at that kitchen table: designing my own album covers and touring internationally!

I used to also fall asleep listening to late night radio; it gently caressed me to sleep but it also acted as my wake-up call the following morning! To me music is indeed one of the highest art forms, expressing the divinity of the universe, speaking to all of us, and is a vehicle for our emotions. It can make us smile, make us angry, it can heal, it can motivate, it can entertain, it can feed your soul. It can make one see beauty.

"When I reflect on the influence music has had on my life and how it's affected me, I'm transported back to the first time, aged seven in Havana, Cuba when my mother started having guitar lessons on a Cuban made Spanish guitar," says Roxy Music guitarist Phil Manzanera on how music shaped his life. "I still have it in my music room and the sound it makes transports me back to my childhood and time spent with my mother.

"It not only has a calming and nostalgic effect but the frequencies that it produces when I pluck the strings seep into my brain, and cause a physically calming effect. This is a personal example of how music adds to the fabric of my life and the resonance that those frequencies give out help me, and I'm sure other humans and animals also.

"When playing music whether recording, creating, or performing, it's as if I am transported into a kind of trance, a kind of meditation where I am 'in the moment' and time is suspended. It helps me mentally and physically. Depending on my mood I play different genres of music to calm or excite me if I want to relax or dance or do exercise. I know that music uplifts my spirits and makes me feel better. I recognise the power of music and that's why I'm so happy to have had a life immersed in music from all genres and from all countries in the world".

That power of music that Phil Manzanera speaks about is what I also realized the moment I first began playing guitar. Not only can it affect the audience, but also the musician themselves. Playing guitar certainly played a major part in building my self-confidence, helping me navigate those important teenage years, helping me understand human nature and, most importantly, connecting me to the spiritual side of life itself.

I remember my first steps on the guitar. A whole new world opened up to me. It was exciting. As I made progress on the instrument my confidence grew along with my thirst for musical knowledge. The feeling I felt once I had mastered my very first song was incredible. I felt like I had reached the summit of a mountain.

To have made it to that first step, as a self-taught guitarist, was an incredible moment in my life. I came to the realization that if I continued to work at it, I could become just like my guitar playing heroes. In those first few years the guitar never left my sight. It was in my hands every spare minute. The moment I got home from work I would go straight to my bedroom, grab my guitar and play until I fell asleep. This ritual continued the next day, and the next. At one point I was practicing up to eight hours a day, that's how dedicated I was. I was willing to put the hours in so that I could become the best guitarist — and musician — that I could be. And the artists I was listening to at the time all played their part in my musical journey.

I didn't care for a social life. I lost myself in my guitar and music, that was my world. That discipline developed and fine-tuned a laser-sharp focus in me. It has held me in good stead ever since and it showed the depth of my passion and dedication.

Years before I took up the guitar, the very first instrument I picked up was the piano accordion. It was a half-sized version that was given to when I was around seven years old by a relative. I remember playing around with it and trying to work out some melodies. I guess that came in handy later when I was older, and when I started tinkering with the piano.

Prior to taking up guitar, I actually started learning and playing the bass guitar. I spent about six months learning it and working with some instructional books, and I got really good at playing bass lines to songs. The instructional book came with a cassette tape that had all the musical examples recorded on it, along with backing tracks where you could practice playing along. The book also taught you how to read music notation. So I learned to both read and play an instrument in that way. But I later realized that without other musicians or backing tracks, to play bass by itself wasn't much fun, nor could someone listening to you playing know what song you were playing unless it was some famous bass riff. That's when I knew I wanted an instrument that could stand on its own, without the need of other players or instruments in order to play a song which people would instantly recognise.

Watching the weekly television music show *Countdown* and seeing all the bands on the show performing to the studio audience, affirmed to me that it was always the lead vocalist or guitarist who stood out the most in a band, and who received the most reaction and attention from the audience. Guitarists always seemed to look the coolest on stage too! They also got the spotlight shone on them when it came time to play a guitar solo. I was sold — hook line and sinker. I traded my bass for a guitar and off I went. My life long journey with the guitar had begun.

My six-string education was also enhanced by my many hours of learning things by ear. I would slow records down so that I could decipher some difficult musical phrase in order to work it out. I think the hours spent doing this and playing along to my records and cassettes was priceless, as it developed my ear and solidified my musicianship which paid dividends for when I finally began playing in bands. Learning to play by ear is by far the most important form of learning that one can do on any instrument.

Singing was also another creative outlet close to my heart while I was growing up. Each day, while walking the few blocks to school from my home, I would lose myself in song, singing aloud the latest song that I had heard on the radio. It gave me great joy. I remember one morning, as I went past one of the houses along the way, an old lady, who was tending to her garden, heard me and said, 'I love your singing voice'.

Another early singing memory I have is from when I was in my first year of high school in 1977. It was just a few weeks after the King of Rock and Roll, Elvis Presley, had died. My parents were big Elvis fans and had many of his records, so I listened to them growing up, but in the aftermath of his passing they were played continuously. I heard them so many times that I began learning some of them. On this particular day our classroom teacher had asked each of us to come up to the front of the class and share something that was of interest to us, with the rest of the class.

Some shared stories of playing their favourite sport, one shared a reading from their favourite book, another shared a simple recipe they had learned, while I simply got up and sang an Elvis song, 'Are You Lonesome Tonight?' acapella! You could have heard a pin drop. After I finished the class burst into applause. It was the first time I had sung in public and in front of anyone, let alone an actual audience!

I was also fascinated by the stories of artists' lives. I remember, in my early teenage years, picking up a copy of *The Illustrated Encyclopedia of Rock* which featured a plethora of bands from the early years of rock and pop music to those of the day, a sort of compendium of their careers and music. I couldn't put the book down. I read it from cover to cover, again and again. It whetted my appetite for more material on the artists and pushed me to seek out, as much as I could, information on the artists I enjoyed listening to.

I would regularly read *Creem* and *Circus* magazines from the US, and *Sounds*, *Melody Maker* and *Smash Hits* from the UK to name but a few. As a music fan I always wanted to go beyond the headline, beyond the myth-making machine. I wanted to know what made an artist tick, what drove them to create, how they approached their sonic canvas, what was their mind set. I wanted a three-dimensional view of the artist and their music, not the one-eyed view that is perceived by the outside world, the taste-makers, the myth-makers, the star-making machine. I wanted to know the real deal. What looks simple on the surface is deceptive as, underneath, a myriad of complexities is always involved: hard work, persistence, tenacity and sacrifice to achieve that goal are just a number of elements that are entwined. It's these human qualities behind it all that inspire, influence and endure.

Being a musician I can relate to, and understand, all of the above, something which has benefited me greatly in my music journalism, in my ability to connect with an artist in a way that a non-musician writer and interviewer may not be able to.

While music is central to my life, it has also been complimented by writing. I love writing. One of the only subjects I excelled in at school was English. Writing essays, assignments and reports spoke to me and was my language to communicate. Books and music were it for me. They moulded my being and character. It has given me the type of life I live. And without writing, music doesn't exist. After all, when creating music, you're also writing music. Even composing music involves writing. You are writing a song, a piece of music. They're mutually interchangeable, as with music, one is telling a story through the aural medium while, when writing a feature for a magazine or writing a book, one is also telling a story through the medium of the written word.

2: On The Road Again

Touring is an essential part of a musician's life. It's not only important to perform live for an audience but to build a wider fan base — a musician must take their music to the people. After all, isn't being a musician all about performing and playing?

One of the biggest misconceptions about touring is that it's a glamorous life of posh hotels, all night parties, seeing the world — a life of wild abandon. Yet the stark realities are nothing like that. Many bands have imploded on the road. Many artists have suffered meltdowns. It's tough and not for the faint-hearted.

It takes a lot of hard work, a huge amount of dedication, sacrifice, money, and an unswerving focus and drive to embark on a tour and, most important of all, it takes a huge toll on you to get through unscathed. I've been lucky that I've toured as a solo act so have a lot of control and freedom to a certain degree on how everything runs, but that doesn't mean it's easier than touring with a band or any easier in general.

Every artist and band starts their touring life huddled together in a van, going from show to show and as their profile and audience builds they will move to the next rung on the ladder, which means they'll have their own buses to travel in (or if you're a superstar, your own plane) and as their career trajectory keeps going upward, they stay in ever more luxurious hotels. By the time they reach the top of the tree, a major artist will have an entourage and a budget provided by their label for tour support, and a daily allowance for the basic necessities, although this is in no way a form of payment or freebie. All costs incurred by the label for a tour are recouped from the artists' royalties and from any profits made from the tour. It's purely a loan to help make the tour possible and run smoothly, as well as making sure it's a successful run, but that loan will need to be repaid in full at some point. Labels are in the business of making money, not granting artists a free ride.

Independent artists like myself don't have that kind of budget, luxury or support. Everything is paid out of our own pockets. On the positive side, this means we are not in debt to any label but, on the flip-side, unless we make money, it's costing us to tour. Any profits made are usually reinvested into the business and into more touring. That is, if you make any kind of profit. The costs of touring are usually higher than what comes back, and in this modern music industry the expenses keep sky-rocketing. Unless an artist is in that small percentage of artists classed as superstars who can sell millions of albums such as Taylor Swift or Ed Sheeran, then the likelihood of gaining financial freedom from purely touring is almost non-existent.

It takes anywhere from six to twelve months to organise a tour. The planning process is slow. Venues need to be booked, VISAs applied for, logistics sorted, travel and accommodation arrangements need to be secured, press organised, tickets need to go on sale, the list is endless.

Then there is the issue of being physically and mentally fit. The road is gruelling and lonely. Only the strong endure and those who have an unwavering drive to succeed, and are accepting of the harsh realities of touring, will survive intact. As with any occupation the possibility of injury or workplace dramas are just as prominent in touring than in a normal nine-to-five job. Though with touring the stakes tend to be much higher since tour cancellations, musician injury, riots and an array of other problems can rear their head at any time and incur financial ruin, lawsuits, and even death. Many artists succumb to the temptations of drink and drugs and the state of mental health can also be affected.

"I once fell off the stage in Louisville, Kentucky at the beginning of Uriah Heep's 1975 American tour and broke my arms in four places, which wasn't very clever," Mick Box, long time guitarist of the English rockers, told me in an interview. "We used to do a song called 'Devil's Daughter' which opened our set and I would run out to the front of the stage with the spotlight on me. I would play the guitar riff, with the pencil light on my hands, and when the band all came in 'bang!' all the lights would be released, so it was quite dynamic. But it was the first show of the American tour and normally the crew would place white tape to mark out where to run out to, so I knew where to go since I was in the dark, but this time there was no mark and I ran out and right off the stage!

"So they picked me up and put me back on stage, gave me another guitar since I had broken the other one, and started again but it was then I realised that I had dislocated my left arm. So I'm playing in a lot of pain and wondering how I was going to get through it and so while singer David Byron was doing a very long introduction, our crew had been down to the hospital and got a nurse, she came in and snapped it back into place and gave me a couple of pain killers to swallow.

"Then there was a bottle of brandy there which we named Dr. Remy Martin, and I was drinking that like water to try and ease the pain and unbelievably I got to end of the show. So we are gathered at the front of the stage to do the bow, and everybody had forgotten about my arm and as we went to bow and leaned in, but I fell down into the pit and broke my right arm in four places! So, they took me straight to hospital and put it into a cast.

"I was getting three injections a night, I was filing down the cast so I could hold my guitar pick. I upped the gain on my amp and got through three months touring that way. The worst thing of all was the inconvenience, as after the show my arm would swell up causing my cast to break so I had to go down to the local hospital and get another put on, then I'd get up in the morning and because my arm would have shrunk from the swelling having gone down it was flapping about, so I had to go back and get another one on in order to do the show. I was on two casts a day! I literally saw every Accident and Emergency department in America. It was horrendous but we got through it. The one thing I did learn, though, was pain management."

Marty Jourard, keyboardist and saxophonist with American band, The Motels, told me of the rigours of the road. "One day, me and Michael Goodroe (Motels bassist) missed some flight in northern Michigan where we had to go from Charlevoix to Traverse City. This was on The Cars tour in 1980 and also on a day off. We somehow missed the regular plane, so he and I had to take this little regional plane that had all the paint worn off it from all the lightning strikes and we thought we were headed for certain death because we were separated from the band, and we were on this thing. I had never been so scared in my life. And it was probably just a typical flight through northern Michigan with the storms and everything, but I was just shaking, and we were both terrified that we were going to die. We obviously did get there and landed safely and went straight to the bar to share with the band and the roadies how freaked out we were."

Putting on a great show entails working under a lot of pressure and if you're an act that has been hugely successful, and is a money-making juggernaut, that pressure is intensified which makes any kind of inner band tension that already exists magnified tenfold. This was the case with the now well-documented Eagles break-up at a live show in July 1980. After becoming superstars with their 1976 album *Hotel California*, which sold in the millions, the pressure to follow-up and build on the momentum was immense, it led to infighting causing the band to implode onstage.

Another example is Swiss heavy metal band Krokus who were under enormous pressure to follow-up on their hugely successful 1983 album, *Headhunter*. Life on the road had aggravated unresolved band issues, as the band's founding bassist Chris von Rohr told me in an interview in 2022. "Unfortunately, after the *Headhunter* album, the band became involved with mismanagement and personal fights, and I was thrown out of the band too," he explained. "Then the band lost the edge, lost who they were, particularly [the band as heard] on those four big albums of ours: *Metal Rendez-vous* (1980), *Hardware* (1981), *One Vice at A Time* (1982) and *Headhunter*. There was too much everything; too much cocaine, too much bad management, too many lawyers and too much bullshit. And success and white powder is a bad combination if you want to keep your head clear."

The endless cycle of writing and recording an album then touring to support it has been common practice within the music industry for decades and it's what keeps the wheels greased for the money-making machine. But by adding touring to the equation when an artist or musician is already overworked from being on this release-tour cycle, further upping the stress and pressure levels, can push anyone over the edge. As Canadian pop-rocker Corey Hart found out when, in July 1987, while touring in support of his 1986 *Fields of Fire* album, he collapsed after a show from exhaustion due to the relentlessness of having released three albums in four years and undertaken two world tours. He was only 25 at the time! Ordered to take time off in the wake of his collapse, Hart heeded his doctor's orders and cancelled the remaining dates to recuperate. Hart's episode highlighted the incredible demands and expectations placed on an artist in order to undertake a successful tour. And it's totally at odds with the public perception generated by the media of life on the road being glamorous.

The logistics involved in a touring enterprise on the scale of stadium acts such as U2, The Rolling Stones or Pink Floyd are undertakings of an almost military type operation. Even then, traversing the globe and performing the same show night in and night out can itself become a chore, one that is in drastic need of spontaneity or of some lighter moments of relief as the following anecdote from blues guitar legend Snowy White, who spent many years as touring guitarist for Pink Floyd, and later for Roger Waters, illustrates.

"The first Pink Floyd tour I did was the *Animals* tour in

1977. I used to walk onstage on my own and start 'Sheep' on the bass guitar, then the band followed on after a few bars. I guess it confused the people in the front rows, trying to figure out who this strange guy was who'd just strolled on. At that time it was a much looser show, and therefore much more fun, than it became later, and there was a fair amount of extended soloing. At one point I actually fell asleep standing up onstage. You know when you doze off briefly and then wake up and for a few seconds you don't know where you are? That was during a particularly meandering piece.

"Another time I was dying for a pee in the middle of the show, so I chose a moment when our two guitars were noodling, and I figured I wouldn't be missed and decided to head for the toilet. In those big places it can be quite a long way, so it was a case of running there in order to get back in time for the next part. I was standing there in blessed relief when I heard someone come in and stand beside me, also in blessed relief. I glanced over — Gilmour! He'd had the same urge. We laughed, 'So nobody's playing guitars then?' 'I guess not!'.

"*The Wall* tour in 1980 was a more regimented affair, due to having to synch with the special effects and the building of the wall etc. The technical side of it was in the early stages, there were no computers etc. It was a case of trying to synch up studio tape machines and video. So it was a learning process for everyone involved, especially the tech guys. That was an interesting thing in which to be involved.

"After I joined Roger's band later on, in 1999, it started off the same way; fairly loose, a band vibe, small venues, testing the water, but as the shows became more successful and the venues became bigger and the special effects became more numerous and important, it became necessary to play to click tracks and time everything down to the millisecond. Nothing wrong with that of course, it makes for a great show, but I occasionally found it difficult to concentrate. I'm not a guy who can play exactly the same thing night after night, I'm not good at that sort of thing, and I would tend to drift off and start thinking about other things, resulting in the occasional glaring mistake which earned me a black look from the boss.

"The final tour I did with Roger, *The Wall*, was an incredible show. I'm not the sort of guy who particularly enjoys being in the spotlight, so I was quite happy to watch the wall go up in front of me. The tours became so big that we were doing stadiums. I must admit I started to miss playing in small clubs with my own band, although I sometimes managed to put some shows together between Roger's tours. From a 60,000-seater stadium playing Pink Floyd material to playing my own music for 100 people in a club a few days later made a nice change."

****

While my own tours of Europe may not have entailed playing to millions or performing in arenas, it was still very much the same route taken by any artist on the touring circuit; boredom, hours of waiting around, flights, travelling, cancellations, exhaustion, and more, are part and parcel of the touring life. Yet what outweighs all the negatives is that one hour or so on stage playing your music to an appreciative audience. The connection between musician and audience and the coming together of a community — nothing beats that. It's one of the most amazing experiences and otherworldly experiences you can ever have. It's the reason why we keep on doing what we do, regardless of how hard it gets. That moment on stage is what it's all about. And will always be about. The following European tour I undertook in May 2014 was my most intense and provides a good insight into what life on the road encompasses.

This European jaunt was undertaken in support of my second full length album, *Terra Firma*, the name translated from the Latin meaning 'solid ground' and took in six countries: Austria, Czech Republic, Poland, Germany, Netherlands, and England over a period of around twenty-six days with twelve shows throughout.

I set off on the long journey from Australia bleary-eyed having arrived at the airport three hours before departure time as is the norm for international departures. Once I checked in I made my way to the airport terminal lounge where we were informed that a slight delay to our flight's departure was expected due to 'seat repairs' before anyone of us could board the plane. I took a seat in the lounge and whiled away the waiting time observing the incoming and outgoing flights on the runway. Other passengers made themselves comfortable, with book in hand and coffee. In one corner a family were deep in conversation, while in another corner, a young couple with headphones on, listened to music. When the boarding call finally came, we queued at the departure gate and were directed to our respective seats on the aircraft.

We then spent another twenty minutes waiting on the tarmac due to strong winds which had caused the closure of one of the airport's two runways, so that only a single runway was now being used for both landing and departing aircraft. After about ten planes in front of us had taken off, the jet engines finally began to roar as we finally taxied to take-off. Apart from some turbulence felt early on in the flight, the journey was smooth and problem free.

Upon arrival for the first stop over in Singapore in the afternoon the weather was hot and hovered around 34 degrees. It was quite a long wait of about seven hours until the next connecting flight which was scheduled just before midnight for the next 12-hour flight to Helsinki, Finland. Staving off the boredom for the long hours ahead, I tried to find a quiet space in the airport, pulled out a book and lost myself in its pages. The tiredness began to kick in, so I tried finding a few vacant seats to curl up and grab a bit of rest, but it was hard to rest in such a noisy environment.

When the connecting flight finally departed it had gone midnight, and there were another fourteen hours of continuous flying ahead. My body was already going into overdrive, the tiredness overwhelming. The only possible solution was to take a sleeping pill, which did the trick, knocking me out for several hours.

I awoke to the glorious blue skies above Finland, the rays of sun seeping through the plane's windows giving me a glorious picturesque view of Helsinki below, of many tiny islands, shorelines and forests and the city itself which was rich in Russian architecture. Thankfully, it was just a brief one hour stop over before my next connecting flight to Vienna. Inside the airport terminal, the heat of the sun's rays pierced through the airport's walls, which made for a very uncomfortable and stifling atmosphere, with whatever cool breeze I could feel, coming only from outside.

Later, as the plane prepared to land in Vienna, there was another magnificent view of the Austrian capital. Outside the airport, and under clear blue skies, my allocated driver updated me on the tour itinerary with news of further shows having been added to my schedule. From there, we made our way to Linz. Now energized by cups of coffee, my jet lag was held at bay and I was ready to face the day ahead. Enroute we detoured for a visit to the 'oldest town in Austria' called Enns, that dates to around 800 AD and had ties to the Roman Empire. I climbed the town's 60-metre-high old clock tower which sat in its main square, before resuming the journey on to Linz.

As the third largest city in Austria, Linz is the capital of the province of Upper Austria and the city sits alongside the Danube, the second-longest river in Europe. Austria is comprised of 46% forest which is protected and, I was informed by a local as a general rule for every tree that is cut down, two others must replace it.

My schedule allowed for one full day of rest to recover from the jet lag and it happened to fall on a public holiday in Austria and Germany, Der Erste Mai (May Day). A day focused on family and community-oriented activities. The roads are completely empty, and all retail outlets close. Usually a maypole is set up in the centre of the town where in the afternoon large street parties take place and much dancing around the maypole.

It being a bank holiday, I visited one of the oldest castles in Austria, Burgruine Ruttenstein. Located about an hour's drive east of Linz and nestled in the Austrian forest, it quietly sits above the village of Niederhofstetten in Upper Austria. The castle dates to the 12th century and incurs a steep climb both by car and foot to reach its summit. Standing upon the castle's highest point, I took in the breathtaking view of the surrounding Austrian landscape. There was a sense of peacefulness and I felt as if my soul was being refreshed by the remarkable beauty that surrounded me.

On the return journey a stop was made to visit a large rock formation which marked an old burial site deep in the forest near Sankt Leonhard Bei Freistadt. The site dates to when the Celts were in Austria. It's an old sacrificial site that is comprised of huge rocks that are clustered together and which are punctuated by small ponds in the rocks themselves that supposedly contain holy water.

The first show of the tour came and went without a hitch; a headlining slot at an 'Akoustic Festival' at a community hall in the Linz district of Solar City, that also doubles as a church on weekends. The festival bill also featured a young German band who had driven ten-hours to perform, and a popular local Austrian band. The success of the first show boosted my confidence and was an encouraging way to kick off what would be three weeks of full-on intensity. By now, my body had finally acclimatised to local time, so the effect of jet lag had subsided.

An early morning rise was in order the next day as we had to board a bus for a four-hour journey to Prague in the Czech Republic. Passing the Austrian and Czech border, the first thing on view was an American casino and building, 'Sin City Night Club'. The journey continued onward through Ceske Budejovice until we finally rolled into Prague, with the city landscape coming into full view with its varied Gothic, Renaissance, and Baroque architecture that underscores the city's strong eastern European connections.

Having alighted from the bus and checked into a hostel

in the heart of the city, it was a short walk to the Hard Rock Cafe — the Prague Cafe was opened in 2009 so it's fairly new and modern — where my next show was performed later that evening. My name was advertised on a huge billboard out front. The city was bustling with people and tourists alike. With a few hours spare before show time I used the time to relax, enjoyed a meal and some drinks and had a look at the rock 'n' roll memorabilia. The Hard Rock Cafe featured a multi-level dining experience with a bar located in front of and below, the main stage of the live entertainment area on the ground floor. Showtime saw me performing two sets of half an hour each to an appreciative audience, who sat and enjoyed the drink and food while listening to the music.

The so-called glamorous lifestyle of a touring artist that is perceived by the public is in stark contrast to the realities of what it really entails as shown by the next morning's events. Needing to shower, I turned the tap on only to find out there was no hot water;l as freezing cold water washed over me, causing me to shiver, I quickly showered and got out of there. When I went to ask the concierge why there was no hot water on tap, they informed me that the hostel had been incurring plumbing problems of late and it was unknown when the issue would be fixed. Having braved the freezing waters, I rewarded myself with a luxurious meal at a nearby McDonalds!

The journey continued onward to Berlin for my next load of shows. Boarding the bus again, it took us from Prague through to Teplice, a large Czech spa town nestled among some beautiful mountains. As we crossed the German border and neared Dresden our bus was suddenly pulled over by heavily armed German Police as part of a random search of passports. It was quite unnerving, as they asked each passenger questions and requested our passports. As I handed mine over to one of the officers, he looked me in the eye and said, 'one moment' and walked out.

After what seemed like quite some time, he returned, walked straight towards me and handed it back to me. In front of us sat a young woman who earlier at the bus stop had asked if anyone could look after her suitcase, which seemed quite a strange request. No one took up her offer. She informed the officer she was from Ukraine enroute to Stockholm. Other officers had now entered the bus and joined in the questioning. They seemed suspicious of her motives and what she was telling them. After they did some further checking with their border police counterparts, she was eventually allowed to continue on with her journey and the bus allowed to finally depart. We lost an hour or so due to the passport checks, but eventually arrived in Berlin almost on schedule later that evening where my German tour promoter met me, and we walked to his home which would be my base for the next week. My sleeping digs was his lounge room floor — no luxurious hotel rooms on this tour!

Speaking of hotels, it reminds me of a story that Dutch guitar player maestro Adrian Vandenberg shared with me about an incident that he once experienced while on the road with Whitesnake in the USA. "The band had just got back into the hotel" he recalls, "and at that time, the touring was quite luxurious because for several years Whitesnake were pretty much the biggest band in the world. Usually, we were not in the touring bus at night for more than 3 or 4 hours. So, at some point in the early morning, you'd arrived in some luxurious hotel like the Ritz Carlton or a Four Seasons. Then you would jump in the shower and jump into the bed and get some sleep. But on one of those evenings, I had just taken my shower, put on my bathrobe on and was ready to go to bed when there was a knock on the door, 'room service'. I thought, I didn't order room service or anything I looked through the peephole and there were two girls in their uniforms with a bottle of champagne on a trolley. I thought that maybe it was a present from the promoter or something because it regularly happened. I opened the door and those two girls jumped all over me and took their clothes off and started ripping into my bathrobe. I was not ready for that at all, and it became really noisy, and it was the middle of the night.

"We usually rented like a whole floor in the hotel with a security guy at the elevator. And so here we were on the floor and the security guy supplied by the hotel saw the two girls, half naked and their uniforms scattered on the floor in the hallway and assumed that I was assaulting those girls because I was one of those long-haired guys! So, he pulled me by the hair into the hallway and I was going, 'No, you've got the wrong guy!' So the girls ran away and our crew manager, who was staying in a room a couple of rooms away, heard the noise, opened his door, and yelled, 'Stop! Stop! He's in the band!'

"By this time the girls had already escaped and the next morning they found the rest of the uniform that they had apparently stolen from one of the carts downstairs earlier in the evening after they had snuck into the hotel and pretended to be room service girls. It was a pretty bad situation because being pulled by my hair across the floor like that… it was a serious moment. The next day, the security guy came to me and apologized for his mistake."

****

My German tour promoter was fluent in several languages: Russian, German and English, and lived in an apartment style building and worked out of a makeshift office in his lounge, the same room that now doubled as my sleeping quarters! The building is in the neighbourhood of Moabit which had once been a manufacturing district and sits near the Spree River. The area is home to many Turkish and Arabic immigrants. Each evening I took a walk to the local Turkish restaurant around the corner that served up a nice, tasty meal on a budget.

With several hours to wait before the evening's show, I explored Berlin visiting Checkpoint Charlie, Alexander Platz, the remnants of the Berlin Wall and other places of historic interest. My first German show was a late minute addition to my tour schedule, a special guest opening spot doing a three-song set of my original material and then guesting with a local blues band who were headlining the gig. A very small audience were in attendance by the time I arrived at the venue, a small dark underground space named Hangar 49 (which closed in 2020), located in Friedrichshain in east Berlin, under a railway line alongside the Spree River.

A row of booths positioned next to the windows inside the space offered up a perfect view of the river. I was told to soundcheck, then take a seat for an interview with a local radio station. The interviewer asked the questions in German which were translated by his assistant who in turn translated my English answers back to him in German. I was impressed with the interviewer as he had researched his questions about me very well. No lazy journalism on his part.

After the conclusion of the 45-minute interview, I was formally introduced to the main band, Don't Tell Mama, a three-piece local blues outfit, and invited to join them onstage for two numbers. The tour promoter warned me that the frontman of the band was difficult to deal with, and I soon found that out when he hesitated at first when told I would be performing three of my songs first. Eventually, and after much persuasion by the promoter, he finally relented. My brief set was met with much enthusiastic applause and the main act then took to the stage. When the time came for me to join them on stage, I grabbed my acoustic and played lead guitar on two blues numbers. The evening ended on a celebratory note.

The next morning, with a few hours spare, I made my way to Hauptstraße 155 in the district of Schöneberg and a five-storey building that housed the apartment where David Bowie and Iggy Pop lived when the pair moved to Berlin in the late 1970s in order to clean up spiralling drug addictions. It also provided Bowie with a base for his Berlin trilogy of Krautrock inspired electronica infused albums, *Heroes* (1977), *Low* (1977) and *Lodger* (1979) though *Heroes* was the only album recorded in its entirety in Berlin at Hansa Studios, which was walking distance from the Berlin Wall. The latter two albums featured recordings that were undertaken in France, Switzerland, and New York. Sadly, Bowie died of cancer on 10 January 2016, two days after having just turned 69. In August 2016 a plaque commemorating Bowie's time at Hauptstraße 155 was added to the building. It is interesting to note that the last time Bowie performed in Berlin was in November 2003.

Heading back around the corner to Julius-Leber-Bridge S-Bahn station to board the train back to my Berlin accommodation, I stumbled across a vinyl store run by 75-year-old Harry Jaksch who had run the store since it opened in 1975. Having just visited Bowie's old apartment, I asked if he had any stories to share. He told me that Bowie frequently visited his store and regaled me with a tale of German punk-rocker Nina Hagen coming in and buying an Iggy Pop record. Every square inch of the store was packed with thousands of vinyl records along with CDs, video tapes and cassettes. I found Berlin to be quite a contrast in both light and dark — the difference between old east and west. I can understand why many of the ground-breaking minimalist electronic music sounds have originated from there.

In the afternoon I boarded the U-Bahn to Rosenthaler Platz in central Berlin (Mitte) where my next show was scheduled. The venue was a short walk from the U-Bahn station. Arriving at the venue my name was listed up on the front billboard surrounded by lights. Named Mein Haus am See — which translates as My House at The Lake — the venue was more of a chill lounge cum bar type space than an actual live concert space, with a very retro 70s feel with original period furniture and decor lining the inner walls. It epitomized the Hipster element of Berlin.

There was no stage area, I was to perform in a corner near the entrance with my back to the footpath and street. Having unpacked my gear, I found I had forgotten to bring along any guitar cables. Luckily, a local musician who my promoter had advised me was planning to pop in to see my set, literally walked in at that precise moment, with his guitar case in hand.

Informing him of my cable dilemma, he happened to have a set on him which solved the issue. The small in-house PA was not the best. By the time I kicked off my set, around 100 people had filed inside and, as the night wore on, the place began to fill to capacity. To end my set, I invited the local musician onstage to join me for an improvisational blues jam.

The stage is a sacred space for a musician. Usually, it is constructed in a way that it's raised about the floor and provides a sort of invisible barrier between the artist and the audience. On bigger stages it's also where security roam back and forth making sure that the space is not intruded upon. But sometimes, overexcited fans can cause that barrier to be broken, as The Moody Blues experienced one time at a show.

"We always set ourselves up onstage rather oddly," explained Justin Hayward, The Moody Blues' singer and guitarist, "in that there were five members in The Moodies. There was me and John, kind of on one side, Ray our flute player on the other side, Graeme in the middle and Mike over on Ray's side as well. So, it was two, the drummer and two, with nobody in the middle. And none of us had the courage to take up that middle space. So quite a few things, particularly in the 60s and 70s, were thrown into that middle space. But the strangest thing was a false leg!

"It was a gig where everybody was pressed against the front of the stage. And we could see this guy who was getting very excited with his pals, and he had a false leg that was from the knee down. I noticed that he took it off and started to wave it around over his head. Then later in the next song, he threw it at the stage, and it landed between us. And I looked at Ray and he looked at me. And the roadie came out behind us, and he asked what he should do.

"I shrugged my shoulders and said I didn't know so we let it lay there. A couple of songs later, Ray said to the roadie, 'kick it back'. So, our roadie took a run up and kicked it back into the crowd, which is often what you did with things that were thrown on stage if they weren't particularly desirable or worth keeping. And we genuinely believed this belonged to somebody else anyway. It wasn't a present, so our roadie kicked it back again. And everybody was happy. Nobody went home disappointed as the guy got his leg back."

****

The next day it was onward to Poland for the next leg of my European tour. Departing the busy Berlin railway station late morning, the 90-minute journey took me eastward to Rzepin, making its way through thick green forests. Upon entering Poland and passing the German border near Kunowice in western Poland, border control police boarded the train and strolled through the carriages to conduct passport checks.

Finally arriving at Rzepin, I was greeted by posters advertising my show plastered all over the station's walls. An assistant from the local tour promoter's office was waiting to escort me to my hotel. The hotel was located on the outskirts of town, in a remote and secluded area that faced a forest. The motel cum bar evoked the spirit of an old American diner, with a couple of locals enjoying a game of pool while the TV screens showed American reality programs.

If you stood outside and faced north, it would take you into town, while facing south, it was a stone's throw to the main highway — Autostrada Wolności (Motorway of Freedom) — which runs through Poland, from Berlin to Moscow. You could hear the sounds of vehicles as they passed by. It was a peaceful site, though the hotel room was just big enough to fit two people at best. Rzepin dates to the 10th century and you could definitely feel a sense of history permeating the air. I felt as if I'd gone back in time. By this stage of the tour loneliness had started to set in, though it was only mid-afternoon and I still had several more hours to kill as I waited for my driver to come collect me to take me to my gig.

My show was held at Restauracja Mak, and I was performing on a makeshift stage that was set under a marquee outside in the beer garden. I found the Polish quietly spoken, well-mannered and they greeted me warmly. No one seemed to speak English, and the language barrier caused a bit of difficulty working with the sound crew. The solution to the communication gap was that I would draw pictures to help explain what I needed. After all, pictures do speak louder than words! As I prepared for my performance, the clouds darkened and soon the heavens opened, and heavy rain began pouring down on us all. Everyone scrambled to cover the PA as quickly as possible. Suddenly, the situation looked critical. If the heavy rainfalls continued in that manner, the show would have to be cancelled. Rain and electricity don't make a good mix. Luckily the downpour came to a halt just as quickly as it had started, and the clouds cleared for the rest of the evening. Around 100 of the townsfolk had taken to their seats and excitement filled the air.

The town mayor informed me that they didn't have many artists like myself coming through their town and confirmed that I was the first Australian to perform in their town. What an honour! With a bunch of shows under my belt already on this tour, I'd finally settled into a groove. I hit the stage just as the last rays of daytime disappeared and night began to fall.

Again, I played two half-hour sets of original music with an interval in between. It was an easy and enjoyable gig. The audience were both appreciative and receptive. It's fascinating how music transcends the language barrier. Music has a uniting force. It brings communities together, we become one. An encore was demanded. After the show CDs were sold and posters signed, and many came to thank me for a great show.

A group of older men who sat under a marquee nearby called me over and told me how much they had enjoyed my concert and invited me to take a seat for a chat and share shots of vodka. They told me that my concert was the main event for the town. One man even offered to exchange some weed for one of my CDs! Respectfully his request was declined, and he happily paid for his CD instead. They told me that I was now part of the family. As the night wore on and tiredness began to set in, I said my goodbyes and my driver took me back to the hotel, himself a little worse for wear.

Next morning it was time to depart for the one-hour long journey heading north easterly to Gorzów Wielkopolski for my next show at Bulwar Sports & Music Pub. As we drove off, with the car stereo blaring out my album, the driver put his foot to the pedal and eventually the car got up to 140 km/h, which became quite nerve-wracking as the roads he was taking were not the best or safest at high speeds. In some sections it was only a 70 km/h speed limit and at times the road wound through thick forest. One wrong turn, and in a blink of an eye, it could all end in disaster.

This is another typical hazard of life on the road, something that heavy metal band Metallica experienced first-hand when bassist Cliff Burton was tragically killed when the band's tour bus overturned and crashed in Sweden during their tour there in 1986. It is also something that James Young, guitarist with American rock outfit Styx, recalled in an interview with me, "We had a crew comprised of three guys who were squeezed into a sort of a pickup thing. Then the five of us would ride around in one car with two of us in the front and three guys in the back seat and what have you and a luggage rack on the top. Then we got a motorhome and on one occasion we got caught up in an ice storm in the middle of the state of Nebraska in the States and the motorhome fell over on its side! We were out in the middle of nowhere and fortunately we survived that. But the fellow that drove that motorhome, we didn't have him drive anymore. He never got another turn behind the wheel."

****

Gorzów Wielkopolski is located on the Warta riverbank, Poland's second longest river connecting to the Oder which forms the main international border between Germany and Poland. The city has a totally different feel, with lots of areas seemingly rundown and there's a post-war feel to certain parts with a very Eastern European look and Gothic architecture. Most of the people I came across did not speak English, especially at the hotel we stayed at. It was difficult to try and make much progress as my Polish isn't great! One fascinating find was walking past a giant mural on a side of building wall which represented Gorzów's importance to cassette tapes as it was the largest producer of tapes in Poland and one of the largest in Europe during the 1970s.

The venue looked like any other sports bar cum live music room, with the stage set up in the back room on two levels. Strangely enough, no stage lights were made available, so once the lights went down for the show, seeing my fingers in the dark became a bit hit and miss. The audience were mostly young, which isn't really the demographic my music is aimed at. It felt more of a club and party crowd and not a place for original music. This was confirmed when a group of young women gathered around drinking and being loud, while watching the sports on the TV. It was one of those gigs where artist and venue had been mismatched. But the show must go on, for good or bad. You just need to look at it as character building and part of developing your performing craft and interacting with a hostile audience. As they say, you either sink or swim.

After Poland it was time to return to Germany and head to Hamburg. With a few hours spare while I waited to board my train, I visited nearby Wiosny Ludów [Spring of Nations] Park situated in the heart of the city. It's got quite an interesting history; first established in the early part of the 1900s, it also featured at one point in its existence, a zoo. The park was busy with families and picnics and many walking its numerous walkways. It was a very peaceful and relaxing place to sit and take in the scenery and the moment.

Finally, my train arrived and departed for the four-hour train journey to Hamburg. As it crossed the border over the Oder River an hour later, we were officially back in Germany. At Küstrin-Kietz, border force police came onboard to check our passports again. In Hamburg I checked into a hostel on the Reeperbahn, the red-light district of St. Pauli in Hamburg. The street was a hive of activity which cranked up as evening came. During the duration of my stay there were some wild moments, such as the day a large group of males were lined up against the wall of the hostel's front entrance, with police doing a full search of each individual, that to onlookers looked more like a raid. Then I got a call came from the tour promoter telling me that night's show in Hamburg had been cancelled due to the venue having suffered water damage, which from the tone of his voice, sounded surprisingly suspicious to me. As the venue was only a few blocks away I decided to walk to the venue to check out whether he was telling the truth. Though the venue was closed at the time, there was noticeably no promotional material or advertising of my gig. The building looked in good shape, with no visible signs of water damage. All I could surmise from outside was that there was never any intention of my show going ahead. I felt that, since the promoter was based in Berlin and the venue was in Hamburg more than three hours away, my questions went unanswered. Cancellations are never pleasant nor are they something any fan wants to hear and though the motto is always that "the show must go on", sometimes circumstances are out of our control.

American glam metal group Dokken experienced something similar during one of their European tours. "In '86 when we were touring, we were opening for [German metal band] Accept and we were covering most of the continent," bassist Jeff Pilson told me. "Then we were just about to head to Scandinavia when Chernobyl hit. And so, we were on our way to Copenhagen to get a flight to fly to Stockholm, and as we were on the way, I ended up getting really sick. I ended up getting a stomach parasite which I got from drinking some water in Germany. This parasite developed on the morning that we were going to drive to Copenhagen and it was a 12-hour bus ride and I had to lay on the tour bus dying of this stomach parasite for 12 hours until we got to Copenhagen. And what we did was, we ended up just cancelling the Scandinavian shows because we heard that the cloud from Chernobyl was going right over Scandinavia. So, we get back to Copenhagen and I end up flying back home to L A. On the airplane, I end up sitting next to a scientist who had just come from Scandinavia and he said that everything we were hearing, it was 23,000 times worse as far as the radiation in the air. And he said to me, 'you've made the right move'."

Back in Hamburg I was disheartened with news of the cancellation, but I wanted to find a way to still perform for my fans and not let them down, so I posted a message on my social media to let my fans know about the cancelled gig and added that since they were expecting a show, especially since one fan had travelled 400 kms to see me, I told them that I planned to set up in front of the venue on the pavement and perform a free mini concert for them. Within minutes of posting, I was inundated with offers from other Hamburg venues offering me their venue as a replacement. One venue called BarRock in Hamburg-Nord near the Stadtpark were prepared to open the venue for me on a Monday night even though they were usually closed on that day.

Word spread and upon arrival at the venue a small crowd were already in attendance awaiting my appearance. The venue supplied not only a good stage area, but equipment and PA and a sound engineer as well. It turned out to be one of my best one-hour sets of the tour. It's these unexpected events that at times can turn the tide of a tour. It also showed me the strength of the German fans support and dedication. German fans can be some of the most passionate music fans around, as Canadian rock band Loverboy found when they toured in what was then West Germany in the 1980s.

"It was in Frankfurt, and we played in what is called the Orderlandhalle, an indoor wooden velodrome where they race bicycles," guitarist Paul Dean told me, "I'd never seen anything like it in North America, so that was pretty exciting from the start. When we finally hit the stage, and after a few songs, we were floored by the crowd, mostly male, (unlike our usual more gender equal audiences), chanting our name, over and over, at full volume. That's never happened before or since in any of our thousands of performances. I loosely compare it to playing in Quebec, Canada, where they regularly break out in what sounds like soccer chants. On one other occasion, we opened for Tom Petty and the Heartbreakers somewhere in Germany, and we were so impressed with the soundman/front of house mixer, that we hired him on the spot. He worked out great."

With the German leg of the tour now completed, it was time to travel to the Netherlands for the Dutch leg of the tour. It was quite a long journey from Hamburg to Sittard via train and bus, with travel taking around six hours. Sittard is in the southernmost part of the Netherlands. At one point as the bus headed towards the Netherlands-German border it suddenly came to a stop at Tüddern, just on the edge of the Netherlands-German border. I was advised that I needed to go to the next bus stop 400 metres away, which would be my last connection to the town. The bus departed and I started walking in the direction advised. But it suddenly dawned on me, the bus stop was not 400 metres away, in fact it was not the right bus stop!

With not a single human in sight, and not sure of my actual location, the clouds began to darken. In the distance I could see a sign up ahead which read 'Welcome to Nederland', I proceeded towards it by foot, but just as I crossed the border from Germany into the Netherlands, the heavens opened! I made a run for it with my luggage and guitar case in tow. It was a mighty downpour. I was soaked.

I managed to make it to the next bus stop intact. I jumped on the next bus, but the driver stopped me before I took my seat telling me I needed to pay my fare even though my ticket clearly stated this part of the journey was included. I explained to him what had happened. He listened and seeing how wet and lost I looked, told me to get onboard. He drove me all the way into Sittard train station where my Dutch promoter was waiting for me to escort me to the hotel in nearby Geleen.

The hotel cum live venue Café de Meister sits in a nice quite area of Geleen, but it was a bit of a lengthy walk to get to the nearest train station whenever I needed to travel. The venue had a second floor that was used as a residence with several rooms, while the ground floor was a bar with a live music stage and area where mostly rock and metal bands from all over the world performed. During the day it was quite serene, but at night it filled with people enjoying drinks aplenty, food and loud live music. It was hard to sleep at times, due to the noisy atmosphere below seeping through the walls.

Once settled in, I was treated to a lovely meal by the house chef with some of the locals invited to join us for drinks and conversation. It was a great way to forge friendships and partake in the community spirit.

My support act for the Dutch shows were a German prog-rock band who I first met and got to know and shared the stage with in Linz on my previous European tour in 2012. They arrived a couple days later and also took up residency at the venue. As a touring musician it's always important to get familiar with a country's traditions, habits and lifestyles and one thing that was surprising find out were the lack of public bathrooms. I found this out one day when I was out and about and needed to heed the call of nature. I asked a local for directions and was informed of this fact. I had to politely ask one of the local restaurants nearby for the use of their toilet.

Show day arrived for the first Dutch show which was held at Cafe De Dwass in Sittard about a ten-minute drive from Geleen. It was a very small intimate venue local; a hive of activity both inside and out. The line-up for the evening featured three support acts comprised of a couple of local acts, my German support band and yours truly as the headlining act. By the time I hit the stage, the place was overflowing with people, and I performed an hour set which was well received with much loud applause.

Show number two didn't require much travel the next evening, except going downstairs to the main bar area!

At soundcheck in the afternoon, the German band were experiencing a dangerous grounding issue with a live wire. At one point a spark of light flashed across the stage area, so it was important to find the issue and fix it. If the problem persisted, the show would need to be cancelled. After investigating, the fault was found which required moving everything to a new mains outlet as an extra precaution. The rest of the evening went without a hitch and the show was a huge success.

The third and final show of the Dutch leg of the European tour was at Muziekcafé Rinie & Nico in Venlo which was about an hour's drive north-east of Sittard. Upon arrival at the venue in afternoon, to our surprise the place was closed and not a single person was in sight. My promoter tried contacting the owner by phone to find out what was going on. There was no mention of our gig on any of the walls outside the building. Eventually the owner's son appeared, apologized for the misunderstanding and opened the venue to allow us to set up. The owner later surfaced too, and it turned out that he was also the chef. Everyone was escorted to a private room at the rear and we each took a seat at a large boardroom type table and were served up a feast of a meal courtesy of the owner.

The venue didn't seem suited for a band performance due to the bad acoustics of the room and so the decision was made to perform in acoustic mode. With lots of older people coming through, I got the impression the promoter had booked the wrong venue for the type of music I and the support band were playing. It felt rather more of a social meeting place for locals than a live performance space. As more people shuffled in, it turned out to be an easy and relaxed performance.

The following day I caught a flight to London for the final show of the tour. It had been an unusually warm summer in the UK with the humidity stifling in the cubicle-sized hotel room I was staying at in Earls Court which lacked air conditioning. The final performance was a late minute addition to the tour itinerary, a brief three song set at Abbey Tavern in Camden. And with that show, the tour was officially over.

The last day before returning home was spent enjoying the sights and sounds of London and catching up with singer/songwriter and friend Steve Harley and his wife Dorothy for a late breakfast at All Bar One, an upmarket, stylish restaurant in Waterloo, where we enjoyed a couple hours together chatting over food and drink.

The returning flight to Australia wasn't without drama. Departing Heathrow for Helsinki for my connecting flight home, we landed to an airport that was eerily quiet and empty with the only people there being those on my flight and a handful of airport staff. We were informed that due to a technical issue, our next connecting flight enroute to Australia had been delayed and no one could give any further update as to when, until at least 3:00 am the next morning. People were visibly upset due to the lack of information and the unexpected delay. We all scrambled to find some seats in the airport lounge in order to get some rest and sleep as it seemed it was going to be a long night and the airport lounge was now our hotel for the night.

Come 4:00 am next morning, and without any notice, we were informed our flight was now ready to depart. In the meantime, my flight from Singapore would need to be rescheduled due to the delay at Helsinki, so I was eventually re-routed on another flight from Singapore, which ended up being a better flight due to having very few passengers onboard. As a result I had a full row of seats all to myself where I could finally get some sleep.

Once back home I was exhausted, and it took a few weeks to finally adjust back to normal day to day life. Also, after having endured a gruelling tour schedule, I weighed myself and to my surprise discovered I had lost 5 kilos which only confirmed the intensity of the four-week tour.

3: Still Got The Blues

Having originated from America's deep south, the blues became the springboard for what evolved into rock and roll. The simplicity of the musical form, with its call and response format which revolves around a repetitive 12 bar structure, makes it the perfect vehicle for storytelling and expressing the melancholic and sombre emotions of the human experience.

The blues is an integral element when learning to play the guitar as it helps develop purity in one's musicianship. I spent several years digging deep into the blues, guitar in hand, studying the greats from the early masters such as Robert Johnson and B.B King to the latter day blues warriors such as Eric Clapton and Gary Moore. Learning the phrasing and improvisational nature of the genre and playing along with recordings played an integral part in helping me develop my rhythm and lead playing and overall musicianship.

Over time my musical tastes evolved along with my skill level and later, as my growing love for pop and rock music got the better of me and as I got more into melodies and the craft of songwriting, I gradually shifted away from playing just the blues. Yet the early years spent within the world of blues were vital and hugely instructive in giving me the starting off point into developing into the kind of guitar player that I eventually became.

Over the years I was privileged to have interviewed many of the blues' guitar playing greats from Gary Moore to Robben Ford to George Thorogood and others. I've also played support in concert to a couple of legendary blues bands, Canned Heat and The Animals, on their respective Australian tours.

In May 2019, sixties Blues legends and Woodstock

favourites Canned Heat returned to Australia to undertake another Australian tour. The line-up for that tour, which took in eight dates mainly on the Eastern Seaboard, was comprised of Adolfo 'Fito' de la Parra on drums and vocals, and newly installed bassist Rick Reed alongside long-standing members John "JP" Paulus on guitar and Dale Spalding on guitar, vocals, and harp.

With 2019 marking the 50th anniversary of the band's blistering six-song set at Woodstock, the band were kept busy with tours of Europe, Australia, Mexico, and Canada. The group has had a revolving door of guitarists come through its ranks during its fifty plus year existence too with Fito, who played his debut gig with the band when they played a show with The Doors at the Long Beach Auditorium on December 4, 1967, being the longest serving member.

The group played their first show of the Australian tour at the Corner Hotel in Melbourne on May 16, 2019. The support slot had been offered to me a couple of months prior by the local promoter. I had just returned home from Sweden the previous day having wrapped up my Swedish tour, and this support show was my first live show back from Europe. Though the effects of jet lag were still hanging around, and due to already being in the groove of touring, I still felt energized and ready to perform again.

Upon my arrival at the venue in late afternoon I walked in just as the band were preparing to sound check. They started playing but had to stop several times because guitarist John Paulus was not happy with timing, and was beginning to get agitated which saw him starting to argue with bass guitarist Reed. Fito was also getting a bit uptight as well. In fact, most of the band, except for second guitarist Spalding, seem to be pedantic and argumentative. After the sound check they quickly walked off stage. The atmosphere felt a bit tense and from what I just witnessed during soundcheck, it was a portent of what was to come later that night.

I walked into the venue's green room located on the side of

the stage. It was surprisingly small with space limited to just the band and myself taking up much of the room. The walls were plastered with past tour posters and indiscriminate graffiti and an old, well-worn couch across the room, enough to seat three band members at most.

I decided to break the ice by introducing myself to Fito.

"Hi Fito, my name is Joe Matera and I am your support act for tonight".

He replied aburptly by asking, "have you a band or are you solo"?

"I'm a solo act and perform acoustically" came my reply.

"That's good and probably better," he retorted.

As I prepared for my sound check, some tech issues with one of my effects pedals came to light. Maybe the vibe of the band's sound check was now rubbing off onto mine. After trying to get to the bottom of the issue, we finally found out that some batteries had gone flat in my acoustic. The sound guy luckily found some spares lying around, tested them to make sure they were all good and gave them to me to replace the faulty ones.

My sound checks are usually short and sweet as I don't have much gear: an acoustic guitar, a few pedals on a pedalboard and that's it. I ran through a few bars of a couple of my original songs, and my soundcheck was done! Returning to the dressing room I found that the band had left and gone upstairs for their meal.

I ordered my meal and ate it alone in the green room along with the front of house person and sound engineer who dug into their meals as well. The atmosphere was nice and peaceful. As it came to opening time I ventured outside to see the audience already queuing eagerly to get in. As I returned the band, along with their tour promoter, arrived back just before I was about to hit the stage and I overheard Fito apologizing to the promoter for an argument he had with him. Apparently Fito had missed two flights the day before and was being castigated by the promoter.

I played a 40-minute opening set to a decent amount of

people and received loud applause, and even some whistles, once my set was done. I re-entered the dressing room and the band asked how it went. The tour manager and sound guy had followed me in and both congratulated me on a 'good show'.

As the lights dimmed, the band made their way to the stage, took their positions and kicked off proceedings with 'On the Road Again' and from that moment, things went south. During the second song 'Time Was', John Paulus broke a string on his Les Paul guitar and had a meltdown, which was very much evident to where I was standing side of the stage. While this was going on, Fito began to introduce the next song as Spaulding took to the mic and announced to the audience that, "We've got a dead soldier up here, not the guitar player, but the guitar!"

Paulus needed to change his string, but when he pulled out some spares he couldn't see which ones they were. Seeing this, the front of house sound guy quickly rushed up onstage, pulled out a torch and shone a light to try and help ease the situation. You would think that Paulus would have had a spare guitar with him, so that when a situation like this arose, rather than trying to waste time and affect the flow of the show, he would just grab the spare and continue playing but no, not Paulus.

In the meantime Fito yelled to Paulus, "take your time!" which from my vantage point was said sarcastically while second guitarist Spaulding took the initiative to improvise a harmonica piece, which quickly saw Fito joining in on drums that eventually segued into 'Have A Good Time'. Finally the crowd, who by now seemed a bit confused as to what was happening, joined in for a hearty sing-a-long. Six minutes later the string change was finally done, and the band were finally back on track and began playing the next song 'I'm Her Man'.

At this point I'd seen enough, and with a vibe of angst still permeating the air, I decided now was the best time to leave — this was a trainwreck awaiting to happen. I found Paulus extremely uptight and pedantic, and watching what was going on from the side of the stage, it was like watching *Spinal Tap*! I felt that this type of vibe would be par for course for this tour with lots of arguing likely to cause the implosion of the band.

A friend of mine, who stayed for the rest of the show, said that later in the set Paulus' guitar again suffered tech issues and Spaulding, now frustrated with the ongoing problems, just gave his guitar to Paulus to play for the rest of the set while he swapped onto harp.

There seemed to be more drama behind the scenes, too. Their tour manager told me that the band had toured Australia the year before and that the promoter did not know about it until it was too late, otherwise he would not have had them back for at least another two or three years. This situation may have further fuelled the angsty vibe of the tour.

Three years later, in 2022, it was reported that Paulus had departed the band due to health issues and was replaced by guitarist Jimmy Vivino better known as arranger and music director for *Late Night with Conan O'Brien*.

****

In July 2022 I was offered the support slot for The Animals on the Victorian leg of their upcoming Australian tour in October and November of that year. I was really excited with the news as I would be opening for one of the truly legendary bands in music history. The band were regulars here with tours in May 2017, Oct/Nov 2018 and another in Nov/Dec 2019. They had been scheduled to return to Australia in 2020 but the pandemic prevented that. Just a month prior to arriving in Australia, the band had just completed a tour of Sweden, Denmark, Netherlands, and the UK.

Heavily shaped by the sounds of rhythm and blues, The Animals earned several Top 40 hit singles on the Australian charts, including a #2 with the now classic 'The House of The Rising Sun'.

This line-up of the band had toured under the name of Animals and Friends in Europe, as Animals' vocalist Eric Burdon owned the rights to that name in Europe but those rights didn't extend to Australia so they were advertised as The Animals for this tour. The line-up for the 2022 tour featured one member and co-founder of the original band — John Steel on drums with Danny Handley on lead vocals and guitar, Roberto Ruiz on bass and Barney 'Boogie' Williams, a fairly recent addition to the current line-up, on keyboards.

The band's Australian tour kicked off at Lizotte's in Newcastle, NSW on October 18. More shows followed at Sawtell, Blacktown, Sydney and Wollongong before the band boarded a plane and headed south to Melbourne for the Victorian leg of their tour. I joined them for their first Victorian show on Friday, October 28 at Sooki Lounge in Belgrave, an outer suburb of Melbourne which sits in the lush foothills of the Dandenong Ranges.

The day had seen nothing but pouring rain and bitterly cold winds, which continued by the time I arrived at the venue late in the afternoon. The venue's eclectic space served as a restaurant, cocktail bar and live music room which easily accommodated around 300 people with standing room only. Tonight was the first of two nights I would be supporting The Animals, and upon my arrival the venue's sound engineer and the band's tour manager were finalising the stage gear for the band to begin their sound check.

With the band's gear now in place, John Steel shuffled into the room, took his seat behind his drum kit, and started sound checking each component of his kit. Once that was settled, Williams did his keys sound check before the rest of the band entered the room, picked up their instruments, tuned up and ran through a song. There was a 5:30 pm curfew in place until 8:30pm for patrons to enjoy their meals and socialise before the live music began. By the time the band had completed their sound check I only had a few minutes spare to set up and soundcheck before curfew.

Once my brief sound check was done, I joined the band in the front restaurant area to sit down and have my meal. They were already around the table tucking in to their meals.

Williams and Handley then grabbed their cigarettes and went outside to smoke them.

With dinner over, it was time to venture downstairs to the dressing room, though calling it a dressing room would be very misleading as it was more of a storeroom for alcohol that was furnished with a couch, a couple of chairs, and packed to the rafters with instrument cases. A crate filled with bottles of wine, beer, water and soft drinks comprised the band's rider and this was placed upon a makeshift small bench. The room was so small it just had enough room for the band and a few others to sit around. With no ventilation, it quickly got hot in there and was stifling.

Handley sat with his headphones on and watched a Netflix series on his phone, while Ruiz sat next him and was also engrossed on his phone. Steel sat next me, and we chatted and, with three hours to kill, I conducted an interview him for a magazine feature. It's times like these that are the most boring of all in the life of a touring musician.

"Some weed would certainly be a good time killer," chimed Handley jokingly before grabbing another bottle of wine. Soon after Handley and Williams stood up and made their way outside for another toke of their cigarettes. There was certainly no privacy the moment you left the confines of the room, as the toilets located outside the room were being shared by band and public alike and at the same time, there was also a private function going on next door.

All this and more were happening in the venue itself, with people coming and going, and strangely enough, children and their parents all dressed up in Halloween costumes roaming about. Curiosity got the better of Handley.

"Why is everyone dressed in Halloween outfits" he asked, "Is it Halloween in Australia?"

"No" replied the tour manager wearily, "they just want it to go on for days".

Steel looked fit and well, and was very agile, relaxed, and happy to share war stories. He told me the band were staying in a hotel right in the heart of Melbourne but since it was about an hour's drive away, it was not worth the effort and time for them to go back to it only to return soon after, so they decided, or should I say, the local promoter decided, that the best option was to stay put at the venue and thus put up with the long hours of waiting around for their show to begin.

They told me they'd just toured Sweden, Norway, UK and recalled a past gig in the Czech Republic where they performed on the rooftop of a presidential building. Steel shared stories of Don Arden and his then assistant Peter Grant — who would later manage Led Zeppelin — and Bob Dylan. He told me of the May 1964 tour The Animals did in the UK with Chuck Berry. At a show at the Hammersmith Odeon Berry, who was famously known for not hitting the stage before being fully paid in cash, had locked himself in his dressing room and promoter Don Arden, along with tour manager Peter Grant, were on their knees passing pound notes under the door to him! Once Berry had received his full amount, he opened the door and walked out with his guitar in one hand and a rolled-up bundle of cash in the other. With every legendary artist I mentioned, Steel would reply that he had either worked with them or knew them — he was a true legend in every way.

One of The Animals most recognizable songs, 'We Gotta Get Out of This Place' had taken on a strong social identification during the 1960s with the cultural air of the times heavily informed by the ongoing Vietnam War. The song soon become an anthem to those conscripted to fight in South East Asia. Written by the Brill Building husband and wife team of Barry Mann and Cynthia Weil, and originally intended for The Righteous Brothers, the song's primary theme was not framed towards a war bent, but more a reflection of a couple wishing to escape small town life for greener pastures. For The Animals it was about escaping their gritty, smoked-filled industrial roots in the North East of England for the promise of a better life, and in the group's case, commercial success in the United States.

The song peaked at #13 on the U.S. Billboard Hot 100. Yet the cleverly crafted lyrics proved to chime perfectly with the plight of young men conscripted to fight in 'Nam.

"When we first released the song in July 1965, the US was just beginning to increase its commitment from 'Military Advisors' to boots on the ground in the shape of the USMC," Steel explained, "and I don't think they were singing 'we gotta get of this place', they were hard core professionals. That would come later when the draftee grunts were pouring in and not enjoying it one bit. By that time, though, The Animals had fallen apart, but it was interesting to imagine all those nineteen-year-olds drunk or stoned singing that song".

When I asked Steel what led to his decision to quit The Animals in 1966, he blamed bad management, endless touring, money issues and the fact he had got married two years earlier. He later re-joined the original line-up for a short-lived reunion in 1975 which led to a brief tour in 1976 and a new studio album *Before We Were So Rudely Interrupted* in 1977, before the band once again imploded. The original line-up reunited once more for a new album, *Ark*, in 1983 which was supported by a world tour before again going their separate ways. Later members would splinter into different incarnations of the group with Steel leading the version known as Animals and Friends.

Did he ever think he would still be touring in his 80s? "I didn't have the faintest expectation back then that I'd still be on the road 60 years on," he told me before adding, "I thought it would all be over in 2 or 3 years."

At one point the venue suffered a power outage and we were all plunged into darkness only for all the power to come back on ten seconds later. Everyone was wondering what the cause had been. By the time I hit the stage at 9pm, the room was brimming with people. My set was well received, with loud applause greeting each song.

With not much room available for storing my gear, I headed out to load my gear back into my car. I was dripping with sweat and the moment I stepped outside, the rain and icy cold winds bit deeply into my warm body, instantly cooling me down, enough for me to grab a thick winter's jacket to keep the cold at bay.

The rain continued unabated as I awoke the next day to the news that "The Killer", Jerry Lee Lewis, had passed away at 87. Today's second show at the Northcote Social Club was sold-out. The pub-cum-live venue came into being in 2004 after a refashioning of the original building, and primarily focuses on putting on shows by niche local and overseas acts.

Arriving with my wife Liz at the venue around dinner time, the band were just ending their soundcheck. Downing instruments, they headed upstairs to the dressing room before making their way back downstairs again and into the bar area to eat their dinner. The bar was a hive of noisy activity and with many either having drinks with friends or enjoying a meal, there was hardly any space available, so the band huddled up around a table in the corner of the pub to eat.

I did my sound check and afterwards ordered a meal which once it arrived, we decided to take a seat and enjoy it in the quiet surrounds of the dimly lit dressing room upstairs. The dressing room wall was adorned with posters of artists and their shows from past performances at the venue. When the band returned, we sat and chatted and I asked Steel how his day had been to which he replied, "shite".

The unusual cold climate we'd been experiencing had been a disappointment to the band as Steel told me, "we can get this kind of weather in England!"

"They expect us to go back tanned," interjected Handley.

I made mention of the news of the passing of Jerry Lee Lewis and Steel recalled a story of how once on a UK tour, Lewis had instructed a guitar player of the band who were booked to be his backing band about the proper way he was to play one of his songs. Obviously annoyed at being asked how to play the song, the guitar player responded with, "I don't listen to your shite music" at which point Lewis turned around and fired the entire band!

I asked Handley how his day had been, and he told us that in the morning he had gone to the local pool where some male fan had turned up wearing transparent speedos showing off, which Hadley described as, "his meat and two veg for all to see!" He also mentioned it being important for him to stay fit while on tour.

Being curious I then asked Williams why he was nicknamed, Barney 'Boogie' Williams, at which point he stood up, undid his trousers, turned around and showed us his bare backside which had the words 'boogie woogie' tattooed across it! "That's why," he answered as he showed us all. We all burst into laughter. The tour manager also joined in the conversation and earlier had told us how much he hated touring, as he missed his family.

When the doors finally opened people started shuffling into the band room. By the time I hit the stage at 9:15 pm the room was almost half full and compared to the previous night's show where most of the audience were older, tonight's audience was comprised of an evenly balanced demographic of young and old which continued to swell as my set progressed.

At the beginning of my set, most present were standing around in the perimeter of the room, hiding in the shadows, but eventually as the numbers increased, they ventured closer to the front of the stage. A small group of people comprised of two men and a woman who were already a little intoxicated, got louder and louder in their conversations which I could hear from my position on the stage. The conversation kept getting louder and continued to do so, the more alcohol they consumed. As my set progressed, the applause after each song also got louder and stronger too, a good sign that I was winning the audience over. Eventually those three people, who by now were smack bang in front of the stage, were now bopping along to my music. When I performed 'Semantics', they started singing the chorus, so I seized on the opportunity and got them to sing along which they did, and the place erupted as I ended my set to much applause and shouts of "you are great" and compliments from all. The 30 minutes I was allocated for my set had passed quickly.

I made my way back upstairs where the Animals were now changing into their stage clothes as they prepared to hit the stage at 10:15 pm. Handley told us that tonight's show was going to be recorded a *Live in Australia* album which they hoped to then sell at future shows. This was the only show they would be recording. Or so they said.

Positioning ourselves off the side of the stage, the band hit the stage and kicked off to play an amazing 75-minute set, they sounded the same as the original line-up had back in 1964. The band began the evenings proceedings with 'Baby, Let Me Take You Home' with the set then going on to feature 'It's My Life', a cover of Jimmy Reed's 'Bright Lights, Big City, I'm Crying' and 'I'm Going to Change the World' which featured Williams on lead vocals. Sam Cooke's 'Bring It on Home to Me' was given a nice airing, as well as, 'Don't Let Me Be Misunderstood' and 'The Right Time' which saw Handley jumping into the crowd and taking a walk through the audience whilst encouraging their participation. This was followed by 'We've Gotta Get Out of This Place' which closed their set to loud applause. When they returned to the stage for the encore, Steel took to Handley's microphone to thank the crowd and say a few words, and formally introduce Handley since he had introduced the other band members earlier in the evening.

Handley's bluesy guitar work was impressive, and his voice a dead ringer for Eric Burdon. Eighty-one year-old Steel played fantastically for his age; he was agile, energetic and played with just as much fire and passion as he had in the early days. When the show ended, they got off the stage and stood in the side of stage area for a minute before returning for an encore. Steel took to the mic to say a few words and asked, "now what could the next song be?" at which point he took his drum seat and Handley commenced playing the famous guitar arpeggio intro to the 'House of The Rising Sun' which whipped the crowd into a frenzy. It was the perfect way to finish their set.

With the show over, they all made their way straight back

upstairs to their dressing room. We joined them as they grabbed a drink. Steel poured himself a glass of wine and after a few minutes and a few sips of their drink, they all headed back down to meet and greet the crowd at the merch desk which was selling Steel's signed drumsticks for $35.

The band had an early morning start the next day as they had to catch an 8:00 am flight to their next show the following evening in Adelaide. The band would be performing a few more shows in the coming week before returning to England. It had been an amazing two days playing the shows and being on tour with the band.

As is the case with performing music, the only way an artist usually receives any sense of acknowledgement from the audience is through ticket, merch and recording sales and the added income that comes from VIP meet and greets. It shows the amount of support and devotion fans have for their favourite artists. As a support act however, the most acknowledgement you can expect tends to come from the audience's applause — if you're going down well with the audience that is. But once you're off that stage there is no more interaction, so you never know how the audience really felt about you. I mean the applause is great but it's just a small token of acceptance and a good marker of whether you've been a success or not as an opening act, but most rewarding of all is when a fan of the headlining band actually tells you directly that they'd enjoyed your music so much that they have become a fan.

So imagine my surprise a few weeks later when I was at my local service station getting fuel. As I walked to the counter to pay a man in front of me in the queue turned around and said, "I really liked the set you played at The Animals concert".

It surprised me so much, I asked him, "oh, you saw the show? So, are you a local then?"

"No" came his swift reply, "I'm just passing through town and stopped to get fuel and I recognized your face".

I thanked him for the comment and told him I was happy to hear he had enjoyed my music. Then, as he was walked back to his car, he stopped suddenly, turned around and came back towards me and said, "and make sure you continue making that great music!" which, as an artist and musician, is one of the most rewarding responses you could ever receive. What made it even more meaningful was the fact he was just passing through and just happened to cross my path. After all, making music is about connecting with an audience and being part of a community that comes together to enjoy music.

4: Jukebox Heroes

I started listening to records at a very young age. I recall being around the age of four, rummaging through my parents' small but diverse vinyl collection and checking out all the albums. My parents had an old radiogram, which was a wooden cabinet that incorporated a radio and a turntable in the living room. Being Italian immigrants my mum and dad had a huge collection of imported 45s from Italy, the most current releases from the contemporary Italian pop charts. They used to visit a local furniture store run by an Italian that also doubled as a stockist for the latest singles from 'back home'.

One of the albums I constantly played at such a young age was The Beach Boys' *Pet Sounds* album. The harmonies were magical and sounded as though they had descended from heaven. It ignited my love for melodies. I would spend weekends putting on that album and listening to it and singing along without a care in the world. I would lose myself in it. From then on, music became my trusted friend for life.

I was lucky to finally interview Brian Wilson from The Beach Boys many years later, a couple of weeks before he embarked on an Australian tour in December 2002 — his first since 1978. I spoke to him via a phone interview to discuss his upcoming tour to perform the *Pet Sounds* album in its entirety live and his musical legacy.

Speaking to me from Beverley Hills, I found Wilson convivial and open to my questioning, even though some of his answers were brief. This was a changed Brian Wilson compared to the reputation he had previously of being a hard interview subject. Some journalists said that interviewing him was like playing with dice.

Aside from the tour, he was also spruiking the recently

released *Pet Sounds Live* album which was the perfect ice breaker to leading me into asking him about one of the most pivotal albums in my musical life.

"Well, the initial idea came from my manager and my wife," Wilson told me. "They got together with me and said, 'you know, *Pet Sounds* is such a great album you ought to make it for the market today with a new live twist to it'. So, we got our band members together [The Wondermints] for it and recorded it on stage live."

When asked about what sort of memories he had of making the original album back in the 1960s he recalled, "I just remember we had a lot of love to give, and we wanted to put it all into our voices. So we did put it into our voices and it sounded like love. It was my ode to God. I was listening to The Beatles *Rubber Soul* album, and I got so blown out by it, that I had to go to my piano and write an album!"

At one point during our conversation a dog began barking in the background and he excused himself by saying, "one moment" before continuing our conversation. I was curious to ask where the inspiration for the ground breaking sounds of the Beach Boys hit 'Good Vibrations' had come from. "The idea for that main motif came to me because of my mother," he revealed. "She had told me that dogs bark at some people and don't bark at others because they pick up on vibrations from people. Then, later on, Mike Love came over to my house and I started playing some music and he's going 'I'm picking up good vibrations' and instantly got into it. So, we wrote it there and then. It took six recording sessions to do that song. We used a 4-track then when we went to mix it down, we put it through an 8-track, which was the first 8-track ever made." At that point, Wilson broke out into song, singing, "'I'm pickin' up Good Vibrations…" to illustrate his point to me. Even over the phone, his voice sounded rich and majestic.

Discussing the aborted recording sessions for the *Smile* album he confessed, "we threw it away as it was inappropriate music for us and so it will never see the light of day." With the more sunny and upbeat disposition of The Beach Boys music, the darker elements that went on behind the scenes were always a topic Wilson found less comfortable discussing in interviews. Yet, recalling his well-documented battle with drugs and mental illness he was philosophical in hindsight. "I've learned you should not take LSD or any kind of amphetamine pills," he said. "You shouldn't do any of those kinds of drugs. I also learned that I should follow through and not crap out halfway through making an album, but to follow through with the record and make a record." Our conversation ended with Wilson telling me that he was writing material for a proposed new studio album which he hoped would see the light of day sometime in the new year.

****

My father used to have a portable transistor AM radio which sat on top of the family's refrigerator in the kitchen. Each morning when he rose from his slumber, my dad would turn on that radio and it would basically provide the soundtrack to the morning as we performed our morning chores. I've never forgotten that experience as I used to always listen to the tunes sitting in the kitchen eating my breakfast, as I eagerly awaited to the hear what song would come up next.

Imagine my excitement when I finally got my own little transistor radio when I was about eight years old. It never left my side. I used to tune in and channel surf and anything that caught my ear, I would sit and take it all in, listening to whatever song had caught my attention. It was on that transistor radio that I first heard the acoustic tinged sounds of Anglo-American folky rockers America and their songs 'Ventura Highway' and 'A Horse with No Name'. Their music oozed with a breezy soft rock vibe which appealed to me. I think later, when I too delved into my own acoustic music, that sort of vibe certainly permeated my acoustic outings.

When I left school and started my first job at the start of the

1980s, I saved up and bought a boombox which were becoming quite popular in the eighties. It incorporated a tape deck, had a great stereo speaker set up and full range sound and also a radio which included FM, AM and shortwave bands. Shortwave provided me with an ear to the world, allowing me to tune in to remote radio stations broadcasting from different locations and cultures around the world. The Voice of America and the BBC World Service were two of the networks that broadcast via the shortwave frequency. Shortwave was in some way an early form of the internet in the way it opened the door to the outside world, musically and culturally.

As was the norm for many music fans at the time, one would purchase a vinyl record and record a copy onto cassette so that way the vinyl would be kept in pristine condition and you'd never need to worry that it would wear out from constant play. If the cassette wore out, you just get another cassette and run off another copy.

When I was first learning to play guitar I picked up a book titled *101 Songs for Easy* which featured a collection of various sheet music of popular songs both old and new that were simplified with just the basic melody and chords. And as a beginning guitarist, this provided me many hours of enjoyment whilst, at the same time, learning all the chords and how to play the songs. The two songs I've mentioned by America were featured as part of the collection in the book.

Once I learned to play those songs, it inspired me to delve deeper into America's catalogue of music. I eventually went back and picked up all their albums that I had missed along the way and explored their music further.

I tend to go through phases in my life where I will pull out an America album, listen to it for few days then put it aside and it might be a couple months or years later before I will do it all again, depending on my mood or circumstance or taste for music at the time. Sometimes, like we all do, I just want to sort of relive the moments that those tunes will recall for me. Music has a great way to bring up your memories in all their resplendent glory.

At the time of picking up my guitar in 1981, and beginning my lifelong six string journey, America were on the comeback trail, having ended the 1970s on a bit of a low. Their commercial resurgence was due to the song 'You Can Do Magic' (1982), a catchy pop-rock tune written by Russ Ballard who also contributed keyboards, bass and guitar on the track, that was tailor-made for the radio. By this time the band had also morphed into a fully electric outfit after spending the previous decade churning out acoustic-fuelled hits.

'A Horse with No Name' is one of those easy songs you learn when starting out on guitar — it's simplicity at its best. Using just two chords, an Em and a D6/9, which may look sophisticated and difficult, but is actually fairly simple, since it only uses two fingers, it's the same chord progression throughout the song. Learning to play this song was great and really helped developed my feel and timing when I played along to it.

The three original members of America — Dewey Bunnell, Gerry Beckley and Dan Peek — were all sons of American Air Force men who first came together in 1970 having met while their fathers were stationed in England. Bunnell was the only English-born member, while Beckley and Peek were both American. Peek departed the group in 1977 and both Bunnell and Beckley remained the core members of group with hired guns rounding out the outfit both live and in the studio from then on.

In January 2004 the group embarked on their sixth tour of Australia. The Australian leg, dubbed the, *On the Road Tour* was part of a world tour that year. I spoke to Bunnell via a phone interview a week before their Melbourne show. This was the first time I had spoken to anyone from the group. On the day of my interview the group had just landed in Perth. With their first show of the tour due to kick off the day after our interview, Bunnell was still getting over jet lag but had spent his first day in the country sightseeing around the port city of Freemantle, south of Perth, having rented a car for the day.

I had always been intrigued as to the meaning behind 'A Horse with No Name' from the first time I'd heard it as a child. Countless myths had arisen over the years that revolved around the song's true meaning.

"It was obviously inspired by the desert," Bunnell told me, "I was always attracted to the wilderness areas and the outback as you call it in Australia. At the time of writing the song, I was living in rainy old England just outside of London and sort of reminiscing about the desert, so it is pretty well straight ahead in that sense. And it's got a little bit of an environmental message too about saving the earth like in the line; 'Under the cities lies a heart made of ground', and it's a simple enough song obviously with virtually two chords."

A lot of urban legends had followed the band with many of their songs. 'Ventura Highway' was another in a long line of urban tales that claimed that drugs were the song's inspiration, particularly with the song's lyrical line of, "alligator lizards in the air" being the most tellingly.

"The whole drug thing is way overblown," Bunnell told me. "The 'alligator lizards in the air' line was referring to a cloud formation, like when you look at clouds and the different shapes that form. And also on a factual basis, there is a species of reptile with that name, a Californian type of lizard. I do haphazardly at times throw lyrics together and so because of that, they may not sound cohesive. With the whole drug thing, they've even said that 'Horse' because it is also a street name for heroin, must be one of those. But I can assure you, they weren't inspired by hard drugs."

The unique vocal harmony interplay that forms part of the group's signature sound first came together when the original trio were all playing together on the cover band circuit. "We had been in a sort of a cover band [The Daze] at first," Bunnell said. "And so, we would always be picking apart vocals from the stuff we were doing such Three Dog Night and The Mamas and The Papas. We cut our teeth in our early days of the mid to late 60s with that little band. Then of course we applied that to our own writing."

At the time of the interview Bunnell told me they were at work on another album. "We've been working just in his home studio and hopefully we will work with producer Andrew Gold again. We did a Christmas album with him recently [2002's *Holiday Harmony*] and it was such a great experience working with him that we're going to put together some original material. We've got about a dozen songs already and when we've got enough that we're comfortable with, we'll take them to Andrew where he will tear it all apart and replay everything." Sadly, Gold would pass away in 2011.

A week later the group were in town performing at the Concert Hall in Melbourne, a 2,500-capacity hall which originally opened in November 1982. In late 2004, the Hall would be renamed Hamer Hall in honour of former Victorian Premier Sir Rupert Hamer who had served from 1972–81 and who championed the construction of the building.

The night of their Melbourne show happened to occur on the Sunday evening of a long weekend, which is usually when many folks tend to get away from the hustle and bustle of the city and head to the country to enjoy the extra day (Monday) of no work.

Surprisingly the show was well attended with both seated and stall areas largely occupied and the band hit the stage at 8:45 p.m. to perform an hour and 20-minute set. Dressed in faded jeans, white sneakers and suit jackets over t-shirts, America's two mainstays, Bunnell and Beckley and the rest of the band, comprising a drummer, guitarist/pianist, and new bass player Rich Campbell, quickly launched into 'Ventura Highway'.

I noticed that with the first few songs of the set they worked harder to reach the higher register vocal harmonies, with bass player Campbell given the job of hitting those higher harmonies, yet it has to be taken into consideration, that it had been thirty years when those songs were first recorded, but the band did put on an exceptional performance.

At one point Beckley jokingly stated that to those in the

audience that, "we're thinner than your average classic rock band" which caused a wave of laughter to echo across the room. He also affirmed that Australia had just awarded the band a gold record, for their latest hits album *The Definitive America* which had been released back in 2001. He also revealed that over the course of the past 33 years, the band had played between 100–150 shows per year.

When introducing the song 'I Need You' Beckley revealed how he had swiped the title from a George Harrison song that The Beatles had recorded for their album *Help!* (1965), and recalled having met Harrison once and admitting the fact to him, to which Harrison responded with the fact that he too had swiped the title from someone else!

Returning to the stage for an encore to the sound of loud applause, Beckley took to the stage in solo acoustic mode, to perform 'All My Life', before the rest of the band re-joined him for 'A Horse with No Name' which closed the evening to rapturous applause.

It would be another 17 years, in March of 2021 before I would finally speak to Beckley. In the aftermath of the pandemic, he had been staying in Sydney, which had now become his second home as he had married an Australian. As was the procedure with all interviews during the lockdown period, it was conducted via Zoom. And exactly a year later in 2022, I interviewed him again as he was promoting his solo album, *Aurora*. Beckley remembered our last chat from the previous year and complimented me on the article I had written for *Goldmine* magazine, which he had thoroughly enjoyed.

****

Growing up during the seventies, I used to hear The Doobie Brothers regularly on the radio. Since their first Australian hit 'Listen to The Music' in 1972, I enjoyed the band's material and eagerly awaited each new recording. It was quite a surprise when the group's sound abruptly changed in the latter part of the decade upon recruitment of singer-songwriter and keyboardist Michael McDonald. With McDonald onboard it brought a softer, more keyboard and horn-laden sound to the group. Suddenly, McDonald's voice became the defining Doobie sound of that period. It reminded me somewhat of Steely Dan, which due to McDonald's previous work with the Dan, wasn't at all surprising.

First formed in 1970, The Doobie Bros were in the fourth decade of their career when they undertook their Australian *Summer Down Under Tour* that began in late December 2005 and went through to late January 2006. The tour kicked off at Brisbane's Convention Centre before making its way down south to Melbourne a month later in January 2006 where I eventually got to interview and meet the band for the first time.

Prior to The Doobie Brothers arriving in Australia, I had been chasing an interview with the band for many months, particularly with long time founding member, guitarist Patrick Simmons. I finally got a call from their tour manager a week before their scheduled Melbourne show who informed me that, although the band's schedule was very tight, he would try and find a window in their schedule that would allow an interview to occur on the day the band were due to arrive in the city.

Then, two days before their scheduled arrival in Melbourne, I received another call asking me if I would be available to do a phone interview with Simmons while he was in his hotel room in Newcastle, NSW later that day, as the band were performing that night at Newcastle's Entertainment Centre.

We arranged and agreed on a time and locked it in for late afternoon and I advised him I would put in the call to Simmons at the allocated time. But about half an hour later, I got a personal call from Simmons himself asking me if I could do the interview there and then! I replied that it would fine, but I needed about five minutes to allow myself time to set up for the interview. He was fine with that too. So, I quickly got off the phone, readied myself with a recording device, mentally went over the questions I would him ask him, and then called him back five minutes later, all ready to go.

We chatted for about half an hour, and I found him a wonderful, warm and enthusiastic person. He was very talkative and in-depth with his answers. He told me that his young son, also called Pat, was with him on the tour and mentioned that the sound I was hearing in the background of our phone conversation was his son playing his guitar. From the small snippets that I could hear down the line, he already sounded very adept at his instrument.

Two days later Liz and I made our way to the Palais Theatre in Melbourne's beach side suburb of St Kilda to meet up with the rest of the Doobies prior to their performance at the theatre later that evening. A former old picture theatre in with a capacity of 3,000, the Palais is the largest seated theatre in Australia and provided the perfect setting for the band to perform.

The band later arrived at the venue in a Tarago van just before 9:00 p.m. As instructed by the tour manager, we waited around the outside area near the side entrance of the stage door. The band first entered the venue to check on the stage and their dressing rooms. Soon after, the band returned to meet a few selected fans that had gathered with us along with a couple of other invited media people. I introduced myself to Simmons, who wore his distinctive hat, and mentioned our phone conversation. He remembered and greeted us warmly. His 15-year-old son Pat, who was a dead ringer for his father right down to the long hair, was with him. We introduced ourselves to him as well. I found Simmons Jr. very pleasant to talk to, friendly and oozing a warmth of spirit; again, much like his father. And I must admit, what a great way for a father and son to bond than to be out on a world-wide tour together.

The few fans gathered outside with us had also been given the privilege — in other words, a meet 'n' greet' — of meeting the band and taking some photos with them as well as obtaining autographs. After about 15 minutes with us all, the band quickly headed back inside to prepare for the show.

We made our way inside took our allocated seats. Around 9:30 p.m. the band hit the stage to rapturous applause and quickly fired off the night's proceedings with a Doobie classic, 'Rockin' Down the Highway'. The set list for the evening's 90-minute performance, was a greatest hits package of sorts, with songs that included: 'Jesus is Just Alright', 'Dangerous', 'Takin' It to The Streets', 'Take Me in Your Arms', 'Black Water', 'People Gotta Love Again' and 'Long Train' Coming'. During one of the songs during the set, Patrick wandered off stage and made his way through the audience while continuing to perform.

The band returned for an encore which saw them tear through 'China Grove' and on the final song of the night, 'Listen to The Music', Simmons Jr. joined his father on onstage playing guitar and singing a line from the song as well. They were also joined on stage by Phil Manning, guitarist for Australian blues legends Chain, who were the support act for the evening.

Aside from the sax player hitting a few bum notes, and Tom Johnston [Doobie Bros. vocalist and guitarist] suffering a faux pas with the first introductory chord of 'Long Train Coming', a very minor observation on my behalf in the whole scheme of things but as a musician you can't help noticing these things, the show was an enjoyable nostalgic trip down memory lane for the most part.

Thirty-five years on the band still oozed with energy and drive and the members, particularly in the form of Tom Johnston, still had the vigour of young men. Johnston on many occasions during the performance commanded the crowd to get up off their seats and rock out. But being a seated venue, it didn't help matters, though towards the end, everybody did finally rise from their seats and danced the night away.

****

Another group that I took an instant liking to when they first appeared on the scene in 1977 was Foreigner. Originally comprised of English and American members, it was led by British-born founding guitarist Mick Jones who, before forming Foreigner was a member of blues rockers Spooky Tooth and The Leslie West Band.

I was in my first year of high school when the group's eponymous debut album appeared in 1977. I was instantly transfixed upon hearing the music, especially when I heard 'Cold as Ice' with its chugging piano-led riff. And once Jones came in with that blistering guitar solo, it sunk its musical claws into me. I became a fan. The band continued to put out great tunes that rocked with cool melodies, and even though they seemed to soften when they brought out their sappy ballad 'I Want to Know What Love Is', I thought it was just a natural progression that showed the depth of Jones and the band's musicianship. If anything, it further solidified my admiration for the band. I later named my early 2000s covers band Double Vision after the group's 1978 album (and song) of the same name.

I finally met and interviewed Mick Jones many years later in May 2006. The band had just arrived in Australia a couple days prior via Nouméa where the group had just performed a concert. It had been eleven years since the band was last in Australia, where they were touring as co-headliners with The Doobie Bros.

While I was waiting in the hotel lobby for Mick to arrive, one die-hard Foreigner fan was waiting there as well and, upon seeing me, came and enquired as to whether I was Kelly Hansen, Foreigner's vocalist. I replied, "No" and told him that I was there to interview Mick Jones. He apologized for his mistake, but told me that because I looked like Hansen, he assumed I must have been one of the band members, which was an enlightening moment for me. We made some small talk before he returned to hanging around the hotel lobby for the chance to catch a glimpse of his jukebox heroes.

Jones, who was staying at the Promenade Hotel in the Crown Entertainment complex, Melbourne's internationally renowned casino complex, arrived shortly thereafter. We decided to conduct our interview in the quiet confines of one of the Crown Towers' glitzy, glamourous, and spacious rooms textured with marbled sculptures and walls. Jones looked healthy, relaxed and happy, and for someone who was 61 years of age at the time, looked amazingly youthful and ultra-cool. Dressed in black drainpipe denim jeans, a white shirt, and with spiky coloured hair, his wrists were adorned with various silver wrist bands. His tanned face the tell-tale sign of time spent in the sun in Nouméa.

We took a seat on a couch, both of us with a coffee in hand, and we spoke for a solid forty-five minutes, uninterrupted and like two friends chatting about music. I found him to be engaging, passionate, very talkative, and open to everything I asked. It was a delight to speak to him. It was one of the most comfortable and relaxed interviews I'd done in a long while. There is always a danger of meeting your heroes that you could be disappointed by them as people and their attitude, but Jones surpassed all my expectations. I suppose that when I interviewed artists who I'd grown up admiring, there was always an element of being star struck. I'm sure it's a common thing with other interviewers too.

Interestingly, whenever we spoke of the band, the glint in his eyes displayed a new-found enthusiasm for the current line-up, especially after all the drama that surrounded the breakdown in his and former singer Lou Gramm's relationship.

"At the moment having put a new Foreigner back together, it feels the best it's ever been," he told me. "In the waning years of my relationship with Lou, I found that we were going through the motions, and we also had to contend with Lou's illness, which was a major blow to him. I want to get the record straight about this matter. We, that is Bruce Turgon [former Foreigner bassist 1992 – 2003) and I, spent a lot of time trying to help him to rehabilitate Lou but we didn't get very far, let's put it like that."

The relationship had deteriorated so much that Gramm

had been scathing of Jones in interviews he had undertaken in recent years. "All I can say is that I did my absolute best, that I could possibly do to try and support him. And we did. You know, we went out for three or four tours with him. He wanted to go out and I think the fact is, that he could have taken better care of himself and. And unfortunately, he didn't, so it was difficult for us to really be doing it."

Jones told me that the current line-up had been in place for about a year by that time and after that year's world tour, which would take in Australia, Europe and the U.S., they were planning to go back into the studio to record another Foreigner studio record. He added that Jason Bonham (Foreigner drummer) had also now joined in the song-writing process and that they were currently putting together a DVD that would surface sometime in the near future.

Jones spent a large portion of the sixties working in Paris, where he honed his song-writing and six string craft playing in various bands including that of famed French pop idol Johnny Hallyday who was tagged 'the French Elvis'. He even did some recording sessions with a pre-Led Zeppelin Jimmy Page. "Jimmy was fantastic, and at the time he already had a name from his session work. This was like towards the end of the sixties. He was one of those guitar players who just had that extra little thing. He just had a knack of being able to do something a little different than everybody else, and his approach was different too."

I was curious to find out whether his stint in France and the bands he was in before forming Foreigner helped him avoid a lot of the common pitfalls when he formed Foreigner. "With my first band when I was about fifteen, I gradually started to realise that I was more committed than the other guys," he replied. "I was ready to throw everything away and go with the music. They were kind of willing to do it, but they wanted to stay in their in their day jobs. That's what I learned at that early age — that it takes sacrifice. So I threw myself 500 percent into it. And sometimes that was hard for people to understand that you do need somebody who really is the driving force behind the band. By and large some people just can't take on that response and they don't want to. Sometimes they just want to show up and play.

"The last band I was in before Foreigner was The Leslie West Band. And that was the year of in and out hell surviving in a crazy situation, and I thought, well, this is it, I've got to take my own destiny in hand. I knew I couldn't rely on other people making the right decisions for me. So I got a bit disenchanted with all of that and was at that stage thinking, well, maybe I'm just not cut out for this, you know, to be in a band or something. And out of that funnily enough, I suppose it had pushed me so far that I had to decide one way or the other."

Jones was chuffed to hear that I had named my band after one of the band's albums when I brought it up in our interview and he proudly gave me his blessing. I had brought along a printout of my band's logo for him to sign which he happily did, and I also mentioned that when I married my wife, we had used Foreigner's classic romantic ballad 'Waiting for A Girl Like You' as part of our wedding ceremony. This too brought a smile to his face.

At the end of the interview I thanked him and mentioned that I would see him again the next night, where the band were scheduled to play their first show of the Australian tour at The Palais Theatre. Come next evening, I eagerly headed out to the show. Foreigner came on just after 9 p.m. and were firing on all cylinders. As soon as proceedings started technical problems began creating havoc for the band. Bassist Jeff Pilson couldn't get his bass working right until about four or five songs into the set and, in the interim while roadies ran back and forth across the stage trying to sort the technical hitches out, the quick thinking Pilson moved over to a second set of keyboards and played the bass notes on the instrument which sounded just the same as if the bass guitar was being played.

If I may digress for one moment, about fifteen years later when I interviewed Pilson, he recalled this event in vivid detail, as it was one of those live moments he would never forget. "My bass tech apparently, all of a sudden, fell into this drug problem, like, almost overnight," he told me, "and so we started doing the show and about three songs in, my wireless went out and I had nothing and so they were trying to fix it and I could tell he wasn't really thinking clearly, but I didn't have the time as I was right in the middle of a show so I couldn't do anything.

"So, I just went up the keyboard player and said, 'just give me a bass sound' and I just did a bass sound on the keyboards and I played bass on keyboards. I ended up having to do that for four songs because it took them so long to get the bass amp working again as he was so drugged out. And what he did do too was, when he was testing it [the bass], we were playing 'Waiting for A Girl like You' which is a ballad, and it was like, 'clank, clank, clank'. It was just a nightmare. So he got fired after the Australian tour."

Once everything resumed working, and before performing their next song 'Break It Up', Kelly Hansen informed the audience that it was the first time ever that song had been performed live in Australia. The song came off their hugely successful album, *4,* that was released in 1981 and 'Break It Up' was officially released in 1982 as the fourth single from the hugely successful album. Hansen was also the premier showman on the night. On one occasion jumping off the stage and into the audience before proceeding to make his way through the seated venue among the fans. Another time he jumped down right into the seat of the front row and sat next to a female fan and continued singing to her.

Wearing a white 'Dirty White Boy' tee, Hansen later introduced the song of the same name with, "This is for all the naughty girls out there". The band later paid homage to Jason Bonham's father, Led Zeppelin's legendary drummer John Bonham, by performing a blistering version of the Zep classic, 'Misty Mountain Hop'. Bonham's drumming definitely sounded like his late, great father was there playing those drums. It was solid, loud, energetic and powerful. After the song's conclusion, Bonham rose and showed his arm to the applauding crowd, the arm displaying a tattoo of his late father's symbol of three interlocking rings, which famously appeared on the Led Zeppelin *IV* album.

Quieting things down for a moment, Mick Jones pulled out an acoustic guitar and with the band performed 'Starrider'. Upon introducing the song, Jones spoke of the song's inspiration and told the crowd that by listening to the lyrics of the song, it would reveal where his head was at the time. My personal take though on lyrics which go: "*Starrider, rider, rider/ Show me where you are/ Starrider, rider, rider/ Take me to the stars*", seem to be more than anything alluding to an acid trip. But one can only speculate.

The acoustic guitar remained for the next song, a stripped back version of 'Say You Will' that saw Pilson, Bonham and Thom Gimbel (rhythm guitarist/keyboardist) up front lending their voices in a cappella style to the song. Hansen later took us to church in the lead up to 'I Want to Know What Love Is' when he asked us if we could be his choir. The night ended with the blistering 'Hot Blooded', an apt way to finish what was a brilliant night of Foreigner's greatest and best hits.

****

10cc are an English band that, during their run of hits and popularity in the 1970s straddled the musical lines in the way that each new album — and each new song — showed the band's diversity of styles that swung between prog-rock and pop to ethereal ballads and even reggae. It also showcased the band's multi-part harmonies and multi-instrumentation.

My introduction to the band was via their 1975 hit 'I'm Not in Love'. I was blown away by the magical multi-layered harmonies which at the time were unique and something that about six months later would be similarly heard in Queen's 'Bohemian Rhapsody'. Listening to 'I'm Not in Love' I remember trying to figure out what that hushed voice was saying in the song's breakdown. For years I always thought it was saying, 'be questing quiet' before I finally found out it was actually, 'big boys don't cry'. [ED: The voice was actually that of band secretary Kathy Redfern].

They may be tagged as a heritage act nowadays having first formed back in 1972, but they still sound as fresh and energetic as they did back in their heyday. They've lost none of their charm and sheen, with their breathtaking live performance both sublime and ethereal. They've honed their craft for more than fifty years now as a band, and many more years for the band's long-standing co-founder Graham Gouldman who, prior to forming the band, had spent much time as a hit songwriter of songs for Herman Hermits, The Hollies, The Yardbirds and others. 10cc also hold the rare privilege of scoring three UK number one singles sung by three different singers. Their first in 1973 with 'Rubber Bullets' was sung by Lol Crème, then in 1975 'I'm Not in Love' was sung by Eric Stewart and in 1978 'Dreadlock Holiday' was sung by Gouldman.

With more than 30 million album sales worldwide under their belt the band have continued to tour non-stop well into their sixth decade. Last in the country in early 2020 just as the pandemic was taking hold, they've been frequent visitors to Australia since their inaugural tour in September 1977 where the band performed seven shows around the country. This latest Australian tour in June 2023 was dubbed, 'The Ultimate Greatest Hits Tour' and they certainly delivered that in spades when I caught the band's show at the Palais.

After this show, they had four more shows to go before the tour wrapped on July 2 after a month in Australia having performed 21 dates. The band then headed home for a busy year ahead of further touring in Europe and elsewhere.

The Palais was pretty much a full house on the night, and I was seated in the middle row in front of centre, about six rows away which had been reserved for media, though aside from myself, there was only one other media personnel seated.

Graham Gouldman (who alternated between bass and guitar) was joined in this line-up by Paul Burgess on drums, who had been with the band since first joining their touring line-up in 1973 and Rick Fenn on electric guitar who first came on board in 1977, and the newest and youngest addition to the band for the past ten years, Iain Hornal, who sang most of the Eric Stewart and Lol Crème material live as well as playing guitar, bass, mandolin, percussion and keys. The touring line-up was rounded out by Keith Hayman on guitar, bass and keys. The diversity of musical skills from each of the band members was impressive as each took turns on playing multiple instruments. Gouldman was back-dropped by several basses and guitars, while Fenn had a spare guitar behind him.

As the house lights went down, a tape played 'Son of Man' — from the Godley and Gouldman GG–06 project — before the band came on and kicked off proceedings with a thunderous rendition of 'The Second Sitting for the Last Supper'. After 'Arts for Arts Sake', Gouldman took to the mic to share with the audience an anecdote about how the song came about. He raised his eyes to the heavens and thanked his father for inspiring the song which came from a comment he'd made, "Art for art's sake, money for God's sake". Gouldman continued to do many in-between song banters throughout the set as did Fenn. Throughout the show Gouldman also gave song-writing credit to all members both past and present. It was a fun and infectious spirit, and you can tell the band all liked each other, as that energy and vibe clearly came across to the seated audience. The set-list showcased songs that effortlessly shifted tempo and style and we even got the full-length ten plus-minute opus 'Feel the Benefit'.

With acoustic guitar in hand and introducing 'Floating in Heaven' a recent single (2022) written about the James Webb telescope, Gouldman explained how it came to be written and said that upon hearing the song his manager thought that the perfect person to contribute to it, since it was an astronomy-themed song, would be Queen's Brian May. So, Gouldman sent it to him, and May loved it and contributed guitar on the recorded version as well as helped produce it.

Fenn at one point also mentioned how he had joined the band 45 years ago. His guitar playing was on fire, he performed some amazing slide guitar work, and blistering lead solos. Fenn's playing evoked a lot of the melodic side of Pink Floyd's Dave Gilmour.

'Say The Word' was introduced by Gouldman as "an Iain Hornal song" that sounded very much a 10cc pastiche, while on 'Silly Love', Fenn, Gouldman and Hayman with their respective stringed instruments in hand broke out into some Shadows-esque dance steps mid-way through.

On the lush and ethereal 'I'm Not in Love', and with all the band on acoustic guitars, they performed a great live rendition of it with Gouldman's bass line taking a front seat in the breakdown section. The only time any sort of additional electronic device was employed during the set was on this song and only for the "big boys don't cry" section, which filtered through on a backing tape. I noticed the higher vocal harmonies were missing and if they were added to the backing the track, like the band used to back in the 1970s when performing the song live in concert, it would have been absolute perfection, but for what it was, it was a remarkable and inspiring effort. For the set's finale 'Dreadlock Holiday' Gouldman chimed, "you will know this song so join in the chorus".

The encore saw Gouldman introducing 'Donna' as "our first ever single" before Fenn, Gouldman, Hornal and Hayman gathered around a single microphone and performed the song a cappella, before Burgess shuffled onto the stage and popped his head in and did a rich deep voice harmony and concluded the song's final line of "Donna, I love you" in comedic fashion. 'Rubber Bullets' the show's closer, got extended and saw everyone up from their seats. As the band left the stage, a tape of Glen Campbell's classic 'Wichita Lineman' seeped through the PA system as the lights came on and the night was over.

The next day I had a midday interview with Gouldman. I had first chatted with him many years ago in the early 2000s via phone and then a couple months back I did a Zoom chat with him. Now I finally got to meet him face to face. It was a cloudy and very cold Melbourne day when I met up with him. With the previous night's show now under their belt, the band were two-thirds through the Australian tour and had two days off before the next show in Bendigo. When I interviewed him via Zoom those few months back, he gave quite brief answers, understandably as he had been doing loads of press in regard to promoting the upcoming tour but in person he was more relaxed, open and very happy to answer questions more fully and was such a joy to talk to. With a spring in his step and dressed in black, with a full head hair that was now white, for a man of 77 years old he still exuded youthfulness and a deep passion for music.

I met him in the hotel lobby of the swank Oakland Premier hotel in Southbank. We took a seat in the front restaurant area which was quiet and not too busy. I mentioned how great the show had been the night before and if Fenn was still an Australian resident, living in Byron Bay, to which he answered in the affirmative. We covered some interesting topics in the interview. I asked him about having come up through the ranks as a songwriter in the 1960s during one of the most creative periods of the 20th century, especially in the wake of The Beatles.

"I just think the quality of music was a whole lot better as it was a golden era. I don't think you and I will witness that again in my lifetime. Maybe it'll happen again in 100 years, who knows? I mean, imagine listening to The Kinks for the first time, or The Animals or the Stones or The Beatles. Yeah. From my own influences, from the 50s, The Everly Brothers, Eddie Cochrane, Buddy Holly, Chuck Berry, Little Richard, then through Cliff and The Shadows, the skiffle era, which was really important in the UK, then The Beatles. I was talking to Brian May about this as we were of a similar age and everybody of our generation has exactly the same influences. Just think about growing up as a teenager listening to The Everly Brothers, it's like, how lucky were we? And still all those things that I heard, they still inform what I'm writing and what I do today. It's in my blood."

I mentioned to him about how much Hank Marvin was a huge influence on my own guitar playing when I was starting out. Gouldman said Marvin was going to catch up with 10cc at their Perth show which would be the final date of their tour. Then he shared with me a story of how one of his songs came to be recorded by The Shadows. "I had a song as an instrumental recorded by The Shadows back in the 60s, called 'Naughty Nippon Nights'. That was a real accident and well, like a lot of things. I was at a friend's house, and he had a stereo tape recorder, and I had this instrumental idea and I said, 'let's just let's just put it down and see what happens'. And then I think my publisher picked it up and said he was going to send it to The Shadows, and they recorded it."

As a prolific songwriter since the sixties, and as a songwriter myself, I was curious to ask him about his song-writing process and whether music came first or the lyrics? "It comes in all different ways," he said. "A lot of the time, I'm just messing around with the guitar, until something happens that makes me go, 'oh, I like that', and then that kind of creates a mood. The actual creative process is a mystery like when you write something and suddenly you've got this whole chunk of music written. It is like your subconscious is the writer. You're just helping it on its way. Sometimes I'll hear something, like just a rhythm of something that can start the process or sometimes I will have a lyric like when famously, my dad [playwright Hyme Gouldman] did when he wrote the first verse of 'Bus Stop' then gave it to me. With 'Bus Stop' I heard the melody immediately because the words told me what the melody was and that led onto the whole thing. And then the middle part of that song I wrote in my head, the whole thing. Anything can set you up really. It's like if you're a writer, your radar is always on, and so you'll pick up something that you know sets off some creative process.

Gouldman admitted that he loves the touring life. "I love

it. I mean, this Australian tour is five weeks long so that is quite a long time. It's a bit too much, really. But it's been great. And the main thing too is, it's not just that you want to be with good musicians. You want to be with good people. That makes all the difference when you're on tour. And I think audiences pick up on that as well. We do very much enjoy each other's company. When we've got days off, we won't necessarily all say, 'alright, I'll see you in a couple of days,' instead we'll go out together for a meal or something. It's a lot of fun." After about half an hour, the interview came to an end, and I wished him all the best for the rest of the tour and we said our goodbyes.

****

I discovered KISS was when I was in my last year at primary school when a class friend brought into class a copy of their fourth album, *Destroyer*. During our lunch break a group of us would gather around the school turntable and listened to the album. It was a revelation. I was intrigued by the album's cover too, where the band members were all wearing Kabuki styled make-up. For the ten-year-old me, it was like seeing and hearing the arrival of beings from out of space. I was hooked.

Eventually the myths that had arisen around this mysterious band of masked musicians became a talking point. I remember being warned that listening to the group was going to corrupt my youth. Bizarrely, I was told KISS stood for Knights in Satan's Service, which was further emphasised by authoritarian figures of the time. Ironically that same acronym stood for Keep It Simple Stupid. One wonders what other possible combinations could be made from the letters.

Overnight Australia became KISS crazy. It reached new heights when the group announced they would be touring there for the first time in late 1980. Everything went into overdrive. It started to kick into gear a year prior when the group released their seventh studio album, *Dynasty*, a more disco-infused outing, which fitted in perfectly with the musical climate of the times. Then the following year they followed up with *Unmasked*, which itself featured more of a power-pop framework than their previous harder rock sounding template. The album and upcoming tour pushed everything into overdrive.

When KISS finally touched down in Australia in November 1980 for their inaugural tour dubbed *Unmasked*, the country was gripped in KISSmania. Not a single day went by without some mention or news item or photo about KISS in the daily newspapers. As the early eighties came round, that hysteria died down, with their popularity on a mass scale waning somewhat, but KISS still retained a stronghold on their Australian fans which continues today.

I eventually got to interview several members of KISS at various points over the years, beginning first with a phone interview I did with Gene Simmons in early 2002. At the time, Simmons was doing promotional activities for his autobiography, *KISS and Make-Up*. Throughout the interview Simmons, who was calling me from his Beverly Hills home, he was obnoxious, and punctuated many of his curt replies with a sales pitch for a myriad of products which at the time included everything from a Gene Simmons magazine to a clothing line and would end his sales pitches with, "anybody who wants to find out more can visit Gene Simmons dot com."

At various points he would reply with answers unrelated to any of my questioning. I asked him about the many inconsistencies and inaccuracies in his book regarding dates and events. I brought to his attention one example, which stated that in 1980 KISS took Bon Jovi out on their first ever European tour, when in fact it was Iron Maiden as Bon Jovi wasn't around until four years later in 1984. To which he replied, "You're right!" before silence fell over the phone line for several minutes. The silence was broken when Simmons, now clearly annoyed at my questioning, retorted, "Look, the book wasn't written as a statistical thing. It was very much a stream of consciousness. I sat down, started from page one and just went to the end. And if the book is about anything, it's really about a little boy who came from Israel and found the Promised Land in America, that's what it's really about. I mean yeah, I'm in a band and we wear more make-up and higher heels than your mummy ever did, but what it's really about is attaining your dreams and really appreciating it."

I asked him about his memories of KISS's first tour of Australia in 1980 and in typical Simmons style he answered with fond memories of all the Australian women. "And lots of them!" then added, "they certainly make my world go round. The women have always made every day above ground a good day. When you think about it, it's the prime urge, the urge to merge! So, any guy in a band who tells you he's doing it because he's got music in his heart, he's just lying! He's playing in a band because he wants to get laid."

A year later, in 2003, I met and interviewed former KISS guitarist Bruce Kulick, who was a total contrast to Simmons. I had first spoken to Kulick for a phone interview the previous year while he was in Australia on his first ever solo tour, but his busy schedule didn't allow a window for a face-to-face meeting. On that same tour I was given passes to his show but upon arriving at the venue, I was not allowed to enter due to there having been some confusion in communication and so my name wasn't on the guest list and in turn, I missed out.

It was arranged that I would meet Kulick at one of Melbourne's busiest intersections, the corner of Flinders and Swanston. As soon as I arrived, I immediately recognized the very tall Kulick who was walking towards me accompanied by his Australian promoter. After the obligatory introductions, it was decided that we walk to a nearby cafe, to enjoy a lunch together, at a place he had enjoyed on his previous tour.

Kulick and I found an empty booth located in a quiet area at the back of the café, took our seats and perused the menu. With lunch ordered, he handed me a copy of his latest album, *Transformer*, which was issued as the follow-up to his debut *Audiodog* that had come out the previous year. Then I switched on my Dictaphone and began the interview.

At the time Kulick was 49 years old and looked in great shape — the only signs of ageing was slightly thinning hair. I brought up the subject concerning the confusion with my previous attempt at seeing his show and having not been allowed to enter. Kulick profusely apologized to me for the débâcle and promised that the next time he would make sure I got in. And true to his word I got to see his show at the Corner Hotel the following evening.

I asked him what his experience was like during his tenure in KISS. "There were many, many highs of course, because we got to travel so much to so many exciting places," he told me. "The difficult parts of it though were always that you knew you had to fit into a certain role and in some way the success of KISS would entrap the band. I was in the non-make-up era where Paul Stanley was the featured guy and so my role was to be the 'be all guitar player' doing everything from the Ace Frehley stuff to the Eddie Van Halen type playing too.

"Obviously whatever you wanted; it was there for you. Like if you were just looking for girls or looking to get crazy you could do that because, when you're a part of a big band and you're a musician, it's expected of you, right or wrong. But the band always had a very hard work ethic, we paid attention to performing well and working at being the best we could be. I really appreciated their attention to it being a business, although sometimes that did take some of the fun out of it, but at least we were very professional."

How did he feel when the original classic line-up of the band reunited in 1996? "In one way, because I knew that it could happen, I kind of expected it at some point," Kulick admitted, "I just didn't know exactly when. I wasn't overwhelmed with shock if you know what I mean. The fact that it happened while we were doing an album that we were working hard on, which was *Carnival of Souls*, was a little odd but I didn't realize that they were kind of orchestrating the 'reunion' quietly, so I felt left behind. But again, I always expected that at some point they were going to get some big offers to go in and do the make-up thing. And so, they did." After spending a relaxing half hour with Kulick while we both dug into our meals, it was time to wrap the interview. I said goodbye to him and told him I looked forward to finally catching his show.

The show the following evening featured Kulick backed by a local pickup band that included his tour promoter on guitar, playing a set that took in cuts from Kulick's two solo outings, plus a smattering of KISS tracks from the album *Carnival of Souls* and classics such as 'Domino', 'Tears Are Falling' and 'Lick It Up'. Prior to the set, a KISS exhibition along with stall holders offering up numerous KISS merchandise and rarities for sale, kept the KISS acolytes satisfied.

My next KISS adventure occurred in February 2003 when the group teamed up with the Melbourne Symphony Orchestra, for a spellbinding rock meets classical music stadium extravaganza at the Telstra Dome in Melbourne. The event was the talk of the town for weeks on end. I wrote a review of the show which was published in the May 2003 edition of British music magazine *Classic Rock*. The following is what I wrote:

Pairings between rock bands and orchestras aren't new. As early as 1969 Deep Purple were hooking up with the likes of the Royal Philharmonic Orchestra for their 'Concerto' at the Royal Albert Hall. In recent years an increasing number of acts such as Metallica and The Scorpions have successfully fused themselves to rock's musical antithesis. So, it came as no surprise last year when KISS announced their own plans to stage their own take on a Symphony show in Melbourne, home to the biggest and most fanatical KISS followers.

An air of frenzied anticipation intoxicates the 30,000 plus gathered, preparing to witness this spectacle. And they've come from far and wide all over the globe — many paying homages to their Gods of thunder with matching KISS regalia — for this one-off coupling of our larger-than-life rock heroes and the 60-piece Melbourne Symphony Orchestra. It may be KISS' 30th year, but tonight's rock and roll circus is equal measure pompous rock and bombastic classic-ism.

The first set is a trip down memory lane as a back to basics 'Alive' circa KISS rock out a classic six-pack to the faithful. Frehley stand-in Tommy Thayer doesn't disappoint, proving a worthy successor to the Spaceman's crown as he unleashes a barrage of rapid guitar fire that opens 'Deuce'. The response to Thayer is one of total acceptance and of family, with fans giving the thumbs up. But just as things start to hot up, KISS break for a short interval with the crowd now hungrier for more.

A cut down 10-piece grouping of the MSO accompanies a seated Criss as he delivers a highly emotional charged rendition of 'Beth' that opens the next 'unplugged' set. The orchestral tinges bring fresh emotional subtlety to 'Forever' and 'Sure Know Something'. Set closer 'Shandi' sees Stanley messing with our heads by teasingly announcing, 'See if you know this one' as he breaks into the intro of George Harrison's 'Here Comes the Sun' — only to segue into Unmasked's long forgotten gem amidst the sound of ear-deafening applause.

Any doubts about Paul Stanley's recent hip surgery showing signs of slowing him down prove unfounded as the final set shows there's still life in this old dog, his prancing butt shaking antics still very much evident. Backed by the 60-piece MSO in full KISS make-up, KISS fully plugged and electrified, the clichéd finale pulls out all the stops.

Simmons spews blood in the growling prelude to 'God of Thunder' raising the intensity up a notch, while an airborne Stanley takes the stage amongst the crowd. With a pyro display enough to light up a hundred New

Year Eves, along with smoking, levitating drums, and fireball displays of encore of 'Rock & Roll All Night', brings proceedings to a rip rousing orgasmic finale.

KISS never shied from putting on rock extravaganzas and the bigger, the better. Tonight, we wanted the best and we got the best, because these unlikeliest of bedfellows were kings of the mountain.

The next time I would speak to another KISS member was in late 2009 when I was granted a phone interview with Ace Frehley, who at the time was promoting his third solo album, *Anomaly*. Frehley was interesting; with a thick Brooklyn accent, his hearty laughter punctuated our half-hour conversation as I covered a wide range of subjects from his new album to his time with KISS. I was intrigued to get his take on Gene Simmons' consistent claims that Frehley hadn't actually played on some of KISS's classic songs.

"It started happening as early as the *Destroyer* album" he told me, "I had done a guitar solo for 'Sweet Pain' but when I later listened back to the final mix of the album, there was somebody else [Dick Wagner] playing the solo on it. It was stuff like that where they would switch my solos without telling me, which probably led me to eventually leave the group."

He also told me how much he struggled with trying to get one of his songs 'Into the Void' included on the group's 1998 *Psycho Circus* album due to the inner band tensions as Stanley and Simmons wanted the bulk of their songs to take priority. He told me how, after fighting for his song's inclusion mid-way through the recording sessions, it was again rejected by the band, before he put up another fight to have it again included. In the end, Frehley only appeared on two of the album's songs, 'Into the Void', and 'You Wanted the Best' plus a bonus track, 'In Your Face', that surfaced on the Japanese pressing of the album.

One of the most talked about live television appearances by KISS occurred in 1979 when all four original members were on the promo trail for their *Dynasty* album and were guests on late night American talk TV show, *Tomorrow*, hosted by Tom Snyder. The appearance saw an intoxicated Frehley derail the interview into a shambolic and often hilarious affair.

"When we did that interview it was our first really big network interview in America," he recalled. "It was a real big show and had a lot of viewers. I know I was nervous about it, and I really think everybody else was too. I had been picked up at my house and because it was a 45-minute drive to the studio, I just started chugging the vodka."

Recalling that inaugural Australian tour in 1980, he said, "Well, you know, we had some nice cruises in Sydney Harbour," before he burst into a lengthy fit of laughter. When I pushed him to explain further, he chuckled, "Rock 'n' roll!"

With the interview coming to an end, I asked Frehley how best he would like to be remembered. "I am what I am," he mused. "I've never really been anything but a wide-eyed kid from the Bronx who got lucky enough to be in one of the biggest rock groups in the world. I'm just happy that I can give people enjoyment when they listen to the music."

Three years later, in 2012, I spoke to the latest in the line of KISS guitarists, Tommy Thayer, who was on the promotional circuit for the group's album, *Monster.* Having listened to the new album prior to the interview, I found it to be a solid effort by the band who were now on the verge of celebrating forty years together. The album also had a heavier sounding edge to it. Overall, it sounded very much like a cross between the band's *Destroyer* and *Revenge* albums.

"It's great to hear, but you know, people like yourself have kind of compared it to certain things," Thayer responded when I shared my opinion of the album with him. "But to me, I see it as just a great rock 'n' roll album and I have a hard time comparing it to any KISS record, because the band is so different today. I think in a lot of ways the music and the direction you know, are very kind of fresh and new".

****

In May 2017 a two-day KISS Konvention was held at a creative hub in inner suburban Brunswick. The event saw much of the space and rooms at the hub taken up by live music, workshops, merchandise, and other activities and was headlined by original KISS drummer Peter Criss in his last ever live performance in Australia. The event also featured Bruce Kulick along with an American supergroup, Four by Fate, that comprised Tod Howarth and John Regan both of whom had played in Frehley's Comet, the band led by Ace Frehley in the 1980s: Pat Gasperini and Rob Affuso, former drummer with Skid Row. Also, a handful of local acts, including myself, were part of the line-up performing KISS covers.

I was offered the gig several months prior after the event's promoter caught one of my shows in Melbourne. The brief was, I had to perform a set of six KISS covers only and they were to be performed in my own unique way which for me was solo and acoustic. I spent several weeks learning the KISS classics and arranging them in a way that were not only done in my style but also done in a respectful manner to the originals.

First cab off the rank was 'Cold Gin' and, since it tends to be a lot of guitarists' choice cut, it was a no-brainer for me and the fairly simple to remember lyrics were easy to handle vocally too. Plus, the song oozes with a super-charged energy when played on an acoustic guitar. 'Sure Know Something' was another KISS song I've always liked, though I had to change the key to suit my vocal range much more comfortably. 'Talk To Me', an Ace Frehley classic, also worked well on the acoustic guitar. I also chose 'Rock n' Roll All Night' but rather than sing it, as it's such a widely-known KISS song that's been covered many times over, I decided to do an instrumental arrangement of it, as I wanted to approach it in a different and unique way, and doing it as a guitar instrumental worked tremendously well. 'Forever', another bona fide favourite, proved a challenge due to the slick production on the original cut, but again, since my brief was to do my own take on the KISS songs, I did this in my singer/songwriter folky kind of way. Finally, 'Lick It Up', which adapted perfectly to an acoustic guitar setting, especially with that opening guitar riff, which is an instant KISS crowd pleaser, and of course, to a guitarist like myself, a staple of rock 'n' roll guitar.

By the time I arrived late morning at the event, a long line of KISS fans had already lined up outside the hall where Peter Criss was due to arrive. Many were holding KISS vinyl albums and various vintage merchandise. With my AAA pass in hand, I headed to the stage area to prepare for my upcoming performance. The stage was set up outside and with the weather being a perfect autumn day with the sun shining, it was a good match. Elsewhere, the rooms in the building were all being taken up by numerous stall holders selling an assortment of KISS wares, there were also allocated photo and signing areas for those that paid for a meet and greet with Criss. On top of that there were also clinics being held throughout the weekend.

Being third on the bill, my performance was scheduled for early afternoon. I set up, the sound guys got me sorted and I waited around for ten minutes since everything was ahead of schedule. I hit the stage. KISS fans are a hard group to win over, their dedication to their musical idols is second to none and the later artists on the bill were all bands, so as a solo act in acoustic mode I was a bit nervous about it and it was a relief that I was well received. The applause was both rewarding and satisfying. I had been accepted into their holy domain.

Roaming backstage after my performance I caught up with Tod Howarth, and we chatted for a while and stood at the side of the stage watching the next act perform. Whenever Criss was not holding court with those who had paid to see him talk or sign their KISS items, he was being kept away from us all. I never saw him once backstage except for when he was making his way between one building to the next, where the promoter and his team created a human barrier so that Criss could walk without anyone stopping him to say hello. It was fascinating to watch. It was as if the Red Sea had parted and Moses was making his way through.

As the night wore on, those of us who had performed earlier in the day and were not the headlining acts, were escorted away from the backstage area to allow the headlining acts to prepare for their performance. At that point I decided to leave.

5: Gonna Make You A Star

As with any industry, charlatans will always appear to weave their hypnotic spell on those unsuspecting individuals who believe in the promise of a quick result and reward and the music industry is no different in that aspect. Unscrupulous hucksters and shysters have always proliferated in the industry since the dawn of the music industry, but more so since the birth of rock 'n' roll. There are endless tales of managers swindling millions from their artist clients by promising fame and fortune to young naïve dreamsters who desperately want to become famous. There have been many instances, too, when a band has signed to a label with the promise of becoming the next big thing, only to quickly disappear from the public consciousness or be unceremoniously dropped from the label just as the band had begun its ascent.

It's as if the artists themselves end up selling their souls to the devil in pursuit of their craving for fame and fortune, rather than for the passion of playing and performing music. Urban legends are born out of this mythological motif. The 19th century Italian virtuoso violinist Niccolò Paganini and 20th century American blues guitarist Robert Johnson are such examples, with claims of them having made a deal with the devil in return for masterful musicianship. In Johnson's case, it's become part of blues music lore that he did a deal with the devil at the crossroads.

Young bands hungry for fame and fortune and the spoils of commercial success who desperately seek that nice fat advance are usually unaware that it's actually a loan against royalties that needs to be paid back. It's not a reward for having signed on or any kind of remuneration for the band. In turn, not understanding the mechanics of the inner workings of the music business they end up losing control of their recordings and career, much to their detriment. It's those who smarten up, understand the many loopholes, put the need to create music as the priority rather than making money that continue to have careers decades later.

In an article first published in 1985 in the *San Francisco Examiner*, and later included in his 1988 tome *Generation of Swine: Tales of Shame and Degradation in the '80s*, the late American journalist and author Hunter S. Thompson wrote:

> "The TV business is uglier than most things. It is normally perceived as some kind of cruel and shallow money trench through the heart of the journalism industry, a long plastic hallway where thieves and pimps run free and good men die like dogs, for no good reason."

And while Thompson was describing the television industry, the description fits perfectly for the music industry. Both are entertainment industries and from my own experiences, and from those of my fellow musicians and artists, it's an appropriate and accurate description. In fact, for years this quote has been used as a meme circulating on the internet, though some of the words have been bent into shape to make it fit the music industry. On occasion I've be offered opportunities to interview the new band on the block, the band that the label is hyping as the next big thing, only to find months later that that same band have been discarded for, ironically, the next big thing, with the cycle ever repeating itself.

One such group that were hyped with big things expected were doubleDrive, an American band that formed in Atlanta in 1996. A few years later in 1999 they released their debut album *1000 Yard Stare* via MCA Records. The band recorded a second album, but upon completion parted ways with their label. They eventually secured another deal with a new label, Roadrunner Records. The label instructed the band to return to the studio where the group recorded four new tracks, reworked two tracks from the completed but unreleased second album, and from that same album selected five tracks to be remixed. The end result, recorded over a ten-day period, was *Blue in The Face* which was issued in April 2003.

In August 2003 the band visited Australia on promotional duties to support the album and to perform a showcase. I arrived at the Prince of Wales hotel in St Kilda late afternoon to catch the last part of the band's soundcheck. The multi-level hotel which, during WWII, was the headquarters for the United States military forces, first opened its band room in 1950 and has been a major player in the evolution of Australian rock and roll history. From the punk explosion of the 1970s with bands such as the Birthday Party on through the ensuing decades where Australian acts such as Midnight Oil have strolled the stages. It's also been a venue of choice venue for many international acts, with everyone from Prince to Lenny Kravitz all stopping over at the hotel.

The venue had a 6:00 p.m. curfew in place and there were only a small group of people present, mainly personnel from their record label Roadrunner, crew and a few hangers-on. As the band came off stage, I was introduced to the band's guitarist Troy McLawhorn, whom I spoke to via a phone interview a month earlier with the interview having just been published in the local street press. He told me he had read the interview and had copies of it and thanked me for the interview and added, "you made me come across as intelligent".

During that earlier interview he revealed the stalemate the band had found themselves in when dropped by their previous label. "We've been holding our breath so long waiting for this to happen," he said. "Being on our new label has been a very pleasurable experience for us. The first record deal that we had, the label really didn't give us any attention, so we were kind of trapped in the deal and we were at home for like two years, and there wasn't any touring happening. Just writing songs and rehearsing and waiting for our contract to expire, just because they wouldn't let us go."

In the wake of the release of the record the group had been on a gruelling tour of the States that saw them play with bands such as Seether, Trapt and Finger Eleven. Road life is arduous and littered with temptations from the use of recreational drugs to groupies. I was curious to find out how the group were dealing with the pressures of touring and the temptations it presented. "I think I saw all of that seedy stuff way before I ever signed a record deal," McLawhorn admitted. "I grew up playing clubs for a living. Right out of high school I joined a band that was playing cover songs and touring up and down the East Coast of the United States. The only thing I ever dabbled in though was smoking pot, but it didn't help. And you know, it does get old eventually."

By now the rest of the band Donnie Hamby (lead vocals and guitar), Mike Froedge (drums) and Josh Sattler (bass) came over and introduced themselves. They were all friendly and told me they had arrived in Sydney a week ago and had four days of sightseeing there which included visits to the Opera House and the Zoo. They also performed a showcase while in Sydney, which was similar to the one they'd be doing later that evening. The band's back line was all hired except for their guitars which they had brought along with them. I was to interview McLawhorn again, but Hamby asked if he could join the conversation, "of course," I replied. So, they showed me to their dressing room where we conducted the interview.

The room, located at the back of the stage area, was dimly lit with stacks of CDs and posters lying about, all of which the band would be signing before the show which was part of radio station Triple M's Garage Sessions. As we began the interview, both Sattler and Froedge walked in and they joined in as we all sat around a table having a pleasant conversation. I mentioned to Froedge that he bore a remarkable resemblance to shock rocker Alice Cooper to which the band burst into laughter and agreed with my observation.

"I hope you mean a young Alice," he replied with a smile,

as he began to sign the CDs one by one that had now been placed in front of him by his label representative. At the time of their visit the single 'Imprint', a song which Hamby had co-written with a long-time friend of the band who was diagnosed with terminal cancer, was all over Australian radio. It had also sparked a little controversy regarding a line in the song that raised questions whether the band were another in a long line Christian bands distancing themselves from such labels.

"Are we a Christian band per se? No," McLawhorn affirmed, "the particular line that people are talking about came from a conversation Donnie had with one of our good friends before he passed away. It's a positive song about the things you leave behind on this earth and that hopefully you go to a better place after you've passed on from this world. We're not trying to preach to people about God in anyway. I mean, each of us as people have our own beliefs and religion and that kind of thing. But our songs aren't Christian songs, they're not about religion. We are just talking about everyday life pretty much."

As the interview came to an end, it was now 6:30 p.m. and the tour manager had walked in to instruct the guys on the evening's proceedings. He quickly took a photo of us for posterity, and I left them to continue with their signings.

At around 9:30 p.m. the band hit the stage and played a 90-minute set. When the band played 'Imprint', Hamby turned the mic around and pointed it to the audience who sang the rest of the chorus back to him. He looked around to Sattler, and began rubbing his arm with his hand to indicate the hairs on his arms were rising because of that moment. The band finished the set, exhausted and drenched in sweat, walked off stage to the loud applause of the audience.

As with many shows of this ilk, an after-party ensued, yet for the most part this type of after-party, is really about the label and its artist networking with those of the media, the invited guests and any others present. It's nothing more but another 'show', with free drinks for all, though nothing is for free as it's all an illusion of generosity as the cost of those drinks are taken out of the band's earnings and royalties. It is all about the end game, which is to gain that vital support needed from retail, media and the powers that be at radio, without whom the band are dead in the water. Having already frequented similar after parties in the past, I took a pass on this one and left.

Roadrunner were hoping that doubleDrive would emulate the success that the band's label mates Nickelback initiated with their Australian showcases in 2001. They were certainly pulling out all the stops. "I think they [Roadrunner] hope that is what happens," McLawhorn told me. "They spent a lot of time with us before we even signed the record deal. They're very strategic with the moves they've made with this band. And I think they've positioned themselves and us so that we can have success with this album."

Yet before the year was out, and with only 27,000 units sold of the album, the band officially split. doubleDrive had become another casualty of the music business and another name in the long list of bands that fell short of world domination and ended up being a small footnote in music history. Since then, the band have only reunited for two sold-out shows in late 2018.

Exactly twenty years later in August 2023, I caught up with McLawhorn again who was in town touring with Evanescence, a band he had joined on guitar in 2007. We spoke in length about our first meeting back in 2003 and about doubleDrive. I finally got the chance to ask him what led to the band breaking up after that inaugural visit to Australia.

"Neither of our two albums sold particularly well," he began, "I don't know exactly the reason for that as we toured relentlessly. On the first album cycle we did a lot of touring, and we spent all our money staying out on the road. We sold merch to pay for hotel rooms. We ended up leaving MCA and got bought by Roadrunner, as they wanted to put out an album with us, but they were really pushing us in this kind of Nickelback direction, which wasn't what we were about at all. And we tried to kind of ride a fine line of doing what we wanted to do and giving them some of what they wanted. It was hard to do, and I feel the music was compromised because of that in a lot of ways, even though I think there's some really good stuff on that second album, I don't think it's exactly what we would have done without pressure to go in a certain direction.

"Roadrunner wanted us to be commercially successful, but at the same time I feel like after all that work that we put in to try and satisfy them and ourselves, they didn't really put everything behind it to get it off the ground. And that's also frustrating as we'd done all this work to satisfy them and we'd compromised.

"What really broke the band up though is that we were out on tour and in Florida and we had a bad wreck. We were touring the States in a van pulling a trailer with our gear in it. It was very early in the morning, like around 5 am. Our sound guy was also our tour manager, and he was driving the van, so he was taking on a lot. We were going down the highway and we kind of guessed that he fell asleep or dozed off, but he said he didn't. But anyway, he said he was trying to pass a semi and as he went around it, he misjudged the distance of the trailer and the trailer hit the front of the semi and when it did, it just started to fishtail, and it caused our van to just flip end over end and sideways. It was crazy. The trailer came off and our van landed on one of the drum cases as when the trailer started to flip, it was flipping end over end, and it pushed the doors open and the cases flew out.

"All of it ended up on the side of the highway, which was very lucky as no one else was involved in the accident. Nobody got hospitalised or anything. I had some cracked ribs. Our drummer was sitting in a captain's chair behind the driver's seat and his shoulder hit the ground and messed his shoulder up a little bit, but nothing permanent. So, we were on tour with some other band, and they were in an RV and later passed us and saw that we were wrecked on the side of the road. They went down on the highway, took the exit and came back and picked us up. And we loaded all of our gear into a rider truck.

Our tour manager then got the police to take him to a place so he could rent a truck 'cause they were like, 'you got to get your stuff off the highway'. So, we loaded it all up and then we played the show that night and that was our last show."

Ron Burman, who was Vice President of A&R at Roadrunner Records at the time and who signed doubleDrive, offered his thoughts on the whole saga. "I don't think we marketed them particularly the same as Nickelback, but we did push them to Active Rock and Mainstream Rock where Nickelback had tons of success at that genre and worked it hard. Our head of promotion, Dave Loncao, loved the band and also loved and believed in the song. He thought it was going to be a slam dunk. We were hoping to get more support from some of the stations that supported their previous singles on MCA like WJRR in Orlando and then unfortunately that station's programmer died I believe and then that main supporter didn't have the champion at the station and didn't really play and support 'Imprint', and we were counting on that to be one of the initial stations to launch it. Unfortunately, the song didn't get the traction and support from the rock radio panel that we were all hoping for and it never took off. We spent a lot of time, energy and dollars on it and it just didn't happen. We were all disappointed about that at the time and as their A&R guy I was crushed as I thought they were also surely going to be a huge band to follow our Nickelback success."

In the aftermath of their last show, and adding salt to the wound, McLawhorn was also now facing a lawsuit. "My wife, who was my girlfriend at the time, came and drove down to Florida from Atlanta where we lived and picked me up and drove me back home because we didn't have a way to get home because the van was destroyed. And because the van was in my name, the rental company were trying to sue me for the van, it was a mess. It had been a tough tour and things weren't going great and I think the wreck was just like, 'we're done'. And it wasn't sad. It just kind of happened and we all went home. And then we all got jobs doing stuff, like the drummer and I were working together, refurbishing houses. And we never did it [play together as doubleDrive] again until the two reunion shows in 2018."

The rock and roll history books are littered with great bands that should have made it but never did, and doubleDrive were just another of those bands in a long list.

"We've seen it many times" says Burman. "In addition to great songs, a hit song and a great charismatic band, you need a lot of luck and timing. There were a ton of good radio rock bands out around at that time and many didn't achieve the commercial success they should have or could have. Again, unfortunately it's the hard knocks of life, in the music business very few get to be huge super stars. They [doubleDrive] were a really good band and lovely guys and I really enjoyed working with them."

****

For the few that may remember Phantom Planet, they're most likely to say, 'oh, wasn't that the band that actor Jason Schwartzman used to be in?' And they'd be correct. Sony Music were pulling out all the stops for this pop-rock quintet from America's West Coast.

The group were first formed while still in high school when they signed a record deal. Comprising Alex Greenwald on vocals and guitar, Sam Farrar on bass, Darren Robinson on lead guitar, Jacques Brauther on guitar and keyboards and actor Jason Schwartzman on drums, their music — on record at least — evoked the laid-back, breezy, upbeat sounds of late seventies So Cal, yet live they were a completely different beast: loud, chaotic, and harder edged.

Schwartzman played a huge role in the band's profile and was a good marketing tool for the record label while Farrar was the son of John Farrar, the singer/songwriter behind many of Olivia Newton-John's chart-topping hits. Such a pedigree and profile certainly helped increase the band's exposure, but would prove to be a double-edged sword, as it proved to be a barrier to the band being taken seriously for their music and not for the profile of its personnel.

Phantom Planet released their debut album *Phantom Planet is Missing* in 1998, and that same year they made a brief appearance in an episode of the TV series *Sabrina the Teenage Witch*. Their second album, *The Guest* was released in February 2002 in the US with the album's opening track, 'California' issued as the lead single. The single would be released in Australia a few months later in May 2002 with the album officially issued there in July. The single would be slow to gain traction and it wouldn't be until it got chosen as the theme song to popular television series *The O.C.* that the band would achieve mass exposure. I really enjoyed the West Coast pop-rock jangly guitar sounds heard on *The Guest*.

The group undertook a promotional visit to Australia in July as part of the album's official release here that same month. They were scheduled to perform two showcases: one in Melbourne and the other in Sydney. Their show in Sydney would see them make a live TV concert appearance on music station, Channel V. I was an invited guest to their Melbourne showcase on July 29, 2002, at the Evelyn Hotel in inner suburb Fitzroy.

In the afternoon of the day of the Melbourne show the band and I convened around a table inside an inner-city café near their hotel where I conducted an interview. The group were enthused at being in Australia and couldn't wait to savour the culture, their sense of humour permeated the whole interview as we chatted in between cups of coffee. "Just because we were born there and raised there, we never actually thought we were Californian sounding," Greenwald told me when I mentioned how much the album oozed very much so of that classic California sound. "We're a combination of all our influences, from The Beatles, the Stones and Elvis Costello, so it's still such a new concept for us to be labelled as Californian sounding".

When I asked if having a famous actor in the group and in Farrar's case, famous parent, proved beneficial, they replied by sharing a story about their flight over to Australia and how each of them had all put their names forward to be considered for an upgrade, but the only person who got upgraded was Sam Farrar. They all concluded that the reason was because, the airline people had seen Sam's name and went, "hmm, John Farrar's son, okay let's give him an upgrade". Before Sam added, "And I really enjoyed the champagne and wine and chicken they served me!" On the subject of acting, Schwartzman confirmed that his next film, *Spun*, was due for release soon, it was a movie he had filmed after the group's recording sessions had wrapped up. Finally, I asked them what they hoped to achieve with the new album, and all were in agreement that their goals were in the short term rather than the long term. They were more focused on making sure that put on their best performance at that their showcase later that evening.

It may have been a cold winter's evening, the chill factor increasing by the hour, where the best place to be was rugged up at home in front of the fire but tonight we were in a queue that started from the entrance of the hotel and ran along the footpath to around the corner, comprising twenty something female fans of Phantom Planet eager to take their position at the front of the stage to catch a glimpse of this hot new band. Anticipation was in the air, and was intense enough to take the bite out of the cold evening air. Eventually we are all packed into a smallish room that held around 150 and, as the background music whiffs through the air, we await the band of the hour.

The band played up to their public persona in style. Their punkish live spirit belied the image the promotional machine pushed to the public. Live, Schwartzman oozed with a spirit that recalled Keith Moon, his highly energetic performance was chaotic at best. The rest of the group exuded a carefree, take no prisoners approach in their stage craft. At times, they rolled on the floor with instruments in hand; they were brash, ostentatious, and the audience loved it and wanted more which encouraged the band to push it to the limit. When the group launched into 'California', the room erupted into a loud chorus of sing-a-long.

In the aftermath of the Australian showcases, the label focused on continuing to push the band and released a follow-up single taken from the album, 'Lonely Day' in September 2002, but it failed to build on the momentum. Phantom Planet's time in the spotlight would be short lived and the big time never really arrived for the group. Schwartzman began feeling being a drummer in the band wasn't satisfying his creative spirit and at the same time, touring began to lose its lustre due to the intense schedule, which saw them tour in support of the album for eighteen months straight and mostly as an opening act. So, midway through the making of the third album the following year, he departed to pursue acting full time. His drumming appears on half of the album's tracks. His replacement in the band was Jeff Conrad.

In 2005, the band made their first feature film appearance, playing a fictional punk band named The Blood Farts in the movie, *Bad News Bears*, which was a remake of the 1976 film, but by then the steam was running out of the band and in November 2008 they took an indefinite hiatus. They reunited for a handful of shows at LA's Troubadour in 2012 before going their separate ways again. But in 2019 the group announced they were reactivating the band and working on new material. In 2023, the group released a new re-recorded version of 'California' signalling a return of the band to full-time duty and a second shot at mainstream success.

I caught up with Greenwald that same year, and we reminisced about that inaugural Australian visit. I asked him whether Schwartzman's profile had proved to have been an albatross for the band. "When he was in the band and we were touring or when the band was just beginning to buzz, that did used to bother the 21-year-old me," he admitted. "It was like 'yes, but there's other people in the band and we've been making music for like a decade already'. In the end, and in retrospect, if you like and know of a band for any reason and you're enjoying the music and going to their shows, and enjoying it then I don't care as any exposure is good."

Looking back at that wild live performance at the Evelyn, Greenwald explained, "I felt that over the course of touring *The Guest* record, onstage things just got good and nasty and fun. One of the philosophies we had as a band was that if you get tired of doing the same thing again, then do it differently."

Twenty years later, looking back on that Australian visit, Phantom Planet guitarist Darren Robinson told me, "In all honesty those Australian showcases are all a blur, but I do remember having a great time. I remember the very long flight to Australia and being remarkably jet-lagged when we finally arrived. I'd been told how intense that could potentially be, and wow that was no exaggeration!

"That trip had a good impact on our band for sure, as it got us out there and allowed us to perform and be seen in front of completely new crowds. But maybe even more than that, it sort of felt like a rite of passage for us collectively. It didn't feel like a 'regular promo visit'."

****

New Zealander's Betchadupa's time in the spotlight was just as short-lived. Having first formed while its members were still teenagers, the group comprised singer/songwriter Liam Finn, guitarist Chris Garland, bassist Joe Bramley, and drummer Matt Eccles and for a time they seemed poised for the big time. Yet their rise to the top never actually happened, with the group soon disappearing out of public view.

The foursome featured two members with legendary musical parentage in the form of Finn, son of Neil Finn of Split Enz and Crowded House fame, and Eccles, son of Brent Eccles, former long-time drummer of legendary Australian rock band, The Angels.

Finn, who oozed cocksure arrogance, which was informed from his privileged background, was the band's leader. Determined to make it big in Australia and the world, the group signed to Liberation Music, an imprint of the famed Mushroom Records Group founded and headed by the late Michael Gudinski. At the time of the group's recording of their second album, *Aiming for Your Head*, in early 2003, the band were touted as the next big thing, a New Zealand musical export to follow in the footsteps of previous successful Kiwi bands that had broken through in Australia and beyond. At the time of having met the group at a Melbourne recording studio, the sessions the band were working on were part of a planned upcoming EP, but later turned into a full-length album instead, and all hopes on that album breaking the band in Australia and opening doors elsewhere. However the expected success didn't appear until a year later by which time the group had relocated to Melbourne from their native New Zealand.

I was dispatched to do a late morning in-studio report in July 2003 while the band were in the middle of recording sessions at Sing Sing Studios. Located in inner city suburb of Cremorne, the red brick studio building was first established in 1975 and over the years international artists such as INXS, Crowded House, KISS, Lady Gaga, and Elvis Costello had recorded there. As mentioned, these sessions were for an EP which would serve as the first outing for the band as part of their new signing with Liberation Records.

Pushing the doors open and making my way inside, I met the band in the midst of recording. Eccles, who stood by the console, decided he was free to do the interview with me while Finn, deep in thought, kept a watchful eye on recording proceedings while the engineer went about his work. Eccles and I were led to another room in the studio complex, where it was a lot quieter and our interview wouldn't be affected by the noisy surrounds.

The band had been holed up here for the past few days and planned to finish recording in another week's time. So far, after three days work, they'd managed to lay down two tracks, 'Move Over' and 'Running Out of Time'. Australian Producer Magoo was helming the sessions and at that early stage the EP remained unnamed with a release scheduled for August-September that year, that was planned to introduce the band to Australian audiences. Midway through our interview Garland walked in, took a seat, and joined in the conversation.

Due to the tight recording schedule the interview was brief, but covered the main points needed for my report. Strangely enough, as we parted both Eccles and Garland went off and began playing a game of table tennis that was set up in the recreation area of the studio. Maybe it was their preparatory ritual before they were needed back in the control room. During my time at the studio, Bramley was nowhere to be seen.

With the interview over, I made my way through the studio's hallway, which was lined with multiple Gold records and as I closed the door behind me, and headed out into the open air outside, Bramley suddenly appeared out of nowhere, running towards the studio, in a desperate attempt to make up for his tardiness.

Their illustrious parentage became a talking point and focus whenever the band undertook media interviews. In fact, many journalists were instructed prior to interviews that questions related to that subject were to be avoided. Both Finn and Eccles were determined that the band made it by their own merits and not because of their parents' reputations. The band showed much promise, but even with the high-profile background that came with Finn and Eccles it still wasn't enough for them and to achieve their commercial goals. The band had also toured with heavyweights Queens of The Stone Age and Pearl Jam during their Australian tours.

After a year in Australia without garnering much traction, the band relocated to London in 2005, to try their luck but things quickly went south. It was no surprise that Finn eventually embarked on a successful solo career in the aftermath of Betchadupa, releasing his debut solo outing *I'll Be Lightning*, in 2007. Though the group never officially announced their break-up, their 'indefinite hiatus' announcement closed the book on the band.

****

Another cause for a band's failure can be the ever-changing popularity in musical styles which can cause an act on the periphery of success, suddenly see them find fame and fortune and vice-versa. Just as fashion goes through trends, music trends are ever-shifting. Since rock and roll was born in the fifties the rock genre has not only evolved but splintered into multiple sub-genres, and these sub-genres splinter into further genres themselves as audience tastes change.

The evolution of musical styles follows a cyclic motion of blending of what's current, with elements of the past revisited, but with a fresh take on what came before at its core. It is also informed by cultural epochs, punk in the seventies for example, was a reactionary response to the economic and social circumstances of the times with its return to basics musical form that echoed the simplicity of the blues structure, and the aggressiveness and energy of sixties outfits such as The Sonics and The Stooges. Leather-clad punk rockers were also evoking the fashions of fifties rockers. What was old became new again. And the cycle keeps going around.

At the turn of the millennium American group The Strokes kick-started a garage rock revival through their debut album, *Is This It* (2001) which featured a cocktail of sounds that echoed the garage rock of the 1960s with the striped down punk-rock sounds of the 1970s. Suddenly, for the next few years, a plethora of similar sounding groups followed suit, and further solidified the movement. And just as it had been ten years earlier, when Nirvana ignited the burgeoning grunge movement causing every record label to search Seattle to sign any band that sounded similar, the same was true in the early 2000s. Just as nu-metal was peaking, the garage rock revival became a much-needed breath of fresh air for a music scene that by then had become a caricature of itself. And the garage rockers of the early 2000s provided the key out of that wasteland.

From Australia, The Vines — who were tagged Australia's Strokes — together with bands such as Jet, The Hellacopters and The Hives from Sweden, The White Stripes and The Dirtbombs from the United States, and The Libertines from England and Franz Ferdinand from Scotland became the leaders of this burgeoning genre.

The Vines had their own share of drama. For example, Vines bassist Patrick Matthews walked off stage numerous times during his stint with the band, eventually walking off for good, largely due to lead singer Nicholls' unstable behaviour and shambolic performances further exacerbated by his predilection for smoking marijuana — he was later diagnosed with Asperger's Syndrome. And there were occasions where tensions were so high within the band that Matthews and Nicholls ended in fist fights on stage. The group's rise to popularity was swift, and their downfall just as fast.

In England, the *New Musical Express* turned its declining sales fortunes around by jumping on these new kids on the block. Each week a new face from the garage rock revival scene greeted readers on the magazine's front page. Just as the late 70s saw music magazines and newspaper give prime editorial coverage to the exploding punk scene, so too did the early 2000s media take a similar approach to this recycling of the past.

Sheffield four piece Hoggboy were one of the bands championed by the *New Musical Express*. The paper claimed they were the next big thing and talked up their "we smoke, we drink, we rock" attitude, a lifestyle the band tried to live up to. Described as a cross between The Stooges, Sex Pistols and The Ramones, they were fast, dirty, and played rock and roll as if they're life depended on it. They were described as a super-charged version of The Strokes.

The four members first met each other on a bus in Sheffield and, having discovered they had shared musical interests, decided to form a band in 2001 with their name taken from lead vocalist, guitarist, and principal songwriter, Tom Hogg.

I first met the band on their one and only tour of Australia in May 2003. They were only performing two headlining shows in the country, one in Sydney and another in Melbourne a few days later. All girl American outfit The Donnas — who also originally sprang from the same garage-punk scene — were also in town at the same as they were touring in support of their major label debut *Spend the Night* and Hoggboy would also play support to The Donnas at their Melbourne show.

The interview with the band was offered to me at fairly short notice and so I was requested to turn up at Liberation Records (the band's Australian label) whose parent company Mushroom also ran Frontier Touring, and who were also touring the band and The Donnas, to pick up a copy of the group's current album, their 2002 debut *Or 8?* to familiarise myself with their music. The office confirmed that the interview was taking place at the band's soundcheck, and I was also given passes to their show.

Hoggboy were playing in the hallowed walls of The Tote, a gritty, sweaty inner Melbourne pub known for giving original bands their first break. I arrived late in the afternoon just as the band were starting to set up their gear for sound checking. After meeting the band's manager, I quietly watched proceedings. In the corner of my eye, I noticed one of the band members sat in the corner, with a Gibson ES-335 guitar laid across his lap, busily putting a new set of guitar strings on his guitar. A glass of beer stood on a table next to him. Having recognized that he was Hugh Smith, the band's guitarist, I approached the mop headed guitarist and introduced myself, "Hi, you're Hugh, right?"

He nodded and smiled, pleased that I already knew his name. He invited me to take a seat while he continued to change his strings and we engaged in small talk. He introduced me to the rest of the band members as they were going about their business on the stage in their preparations. We continued chatting about music, guitars and rock and roll. Once the strings were changed, he handed me his guitar and asked whether I like to have a play of it. I accepted his offer, and my fingers began fretting away. I then handed it back to him and he started noodling away on the guitar. The atmosphere was all spontaneous and very casual.

He told me that back home in Sheffield his father was a folk guitarist, and as such began playing me a finger picking rendition of 'The Entertainer'. He was all smiles and told me it was great to be speaking to another guitarist for once rather than just a journalist. After what seemed like ages, he was instructed to reconvene with his band members, climbed up on the stage and with that, they commenced sound checking.

Extra precautions were taken to ensure the soundcheck and the show went off without a hitch. You see, a few months earlier, while the band were playing a show in Spain, their set was cut short after bassist Andrew Bailey received an electric shock on stage which caused a momentary loss of feeling in his face and blurred vision, fortunately he made a full recovery.

Their sound check comprised the performance of two numbers, 'Left and Right' and a song they'd just written, which Smith later told me was titled, '400 Boys'. Waiting in the wings were one of the three support acts for the evening, Neon, a Melbourne-based band that were also being hyped as the next big thing during the early 2000s 'garage rock revival' phase who were anxiously awaiting their soundcheck. Once Hoggboy's sound check was over, we all made our way to the pub's beer garden where I conducted an interview with the whole band.

"I used to listen to a lot of Velvet Underground, The Jon Spencer Blues Explosion and Sex Pistols," Hogg told me, "Jon Spencer is probably the style I play in the most when it comes to playing guitar. But for the band, the main influences are Velvet Underground, The Stooges and Sex Pistols."

Eighteen months prior to my interview Hoggboy had played shows with The Strokes and The White Stripes which earned them the label of the 'British answer to The Strokes'.

"It was on our second tour," Hogg told me, "and most of the songs on the album hadn't been written yet. We were only doing twenty-minute sets and went down very well in New York. We were given a lot of hype and we probably didn't live up to it, as it was early on and like I said, we hadn't even made our debut album yet."

I asked them about the new song they'd just ran through at soundcheck. Smith revealed the track was slated for a film with the same title with the band also at work on writing further music for the film. "The director of the film came to see us play in London and really loved it," said Smith, "so he asked us if we could write some tunes for it." Smith also said the group were due to head to Canada later that year to film a cameo appearance in the film as well as shoot the official video for the new song, which would later appear on the band's second album, *Seven Miles of Love.*

I brought up the topic of The Vines since they were being championed by the press as the leaders of the new rock revival. The band told me that Hoggboy drummer Richy Westley hated them. Curious to know why, Westley told me that one night he went up to introduce himself to The Vines and, as he went to shake hands with temperamental lead singer Craig Nicholls who threw a tantrum. Westley finished by pronouncing, "Craig Nicholls is a cunt!"

Hogg revealed that on the band's previous slot supporting The Donnas, with the long night ahead of the comedown of having just performed their set, he got smashed. "With our rider we only get beers," he began, "The Donnas rider not only included beer, but they also got bourbon. So, I managed to sneak a bottle from their rider and took it with me back to my hotel room, sat there and drank it."

They continued to share war stories with me, including one about how Bailey ended up in a jacuzzi with two women on the first night of their Australian tour. With the interview over and having made a connection on a musician-to-musician level, Smith offered me his email address and said, "let's keep in touch and talk more about music".

They then left the building to return to their hotel and get some dinner and whatever pre-show ritual they followed in their preparation for their show later that evening. By the time the band hit the stage just after midnight, the room was brimming with a boisterous audience. The band's Liberation/Mushroom record label personnel were all in attendance including Mushroom head Michael Gudinski. Local band Magic Dirt, who were themselves enjoying some commercial success, were also in attendance to check out the band.

Hoggboy kicked off their live performance with the two songs they had played earlier at the soundcheck before throttling their way through a 12 song 45-minute set, comprised mostly of tracks from their debut album and newer material. Considering they were headlining; it was a rather short and frenzied set and very much in the spirit of a live Ramones concert.

Clad in tight fitting black leather jackets and blue jeans, and Smith, with a cigarette dangling from his lips, Hoggboy oozed energy, which evoked the live essence of the Sex Pistols. Unfortunately Hoggboy's debut album, produced by veteran Chris Thomas with a few tracks also produced by fellow Sheffielders Richard Hawley and Colin Elliot, didn't quite capture this energy. Wearing black wraparound sunglasses, front man and band leader Tom Hogg shared spirited banter in between songs and at one point asked the crowd if they wanted to see Bailey's naked torso? The crowd expressed their approval. Next, he asked, "What about if Ricky pulls out his cock for you?" and a roar of approval engulfed the room.

The group finished their performance in shambolic fashion at 1 am to the deafening sounds of an audience shouting 'more', to which the band obliged, returning to the stage to play the encore 'Call Me Suck'. Downing tools, they walked off the stage, drenched in sweat and made their way through the throng of people, many shaking their hands as they passed by and congratulating them on their performance.

Later that same evening (it was now early hours of the

morning) they would be performing another show as support for The Donnas at Prince of Wales hotel in bayside St Kilda. That show had been sold out for weeks prior and the very next day the band were scheduled to return to the UK. It was a fast and furious few days for the band.

A few days later I received an email from Smith telling me they'd landed safely back in England in the early hours of the morning and a few hours later were finally at home in Sheffield. Smith stated that by the time the band were about to depart Melbourne, he could hardly string a sentence together, as the party had never stopped. He told me that the group's support slot with The Donnas turned out to be quite an eventful show, as he had gotten so drunk after drinking vodka and the entire Donnas drinks rider, he had urinated on one of the Donnas crew members who grabbed him and threw him through one of the dressing room's glass shower doors, shattering it. He escaped with just a few minor cuts and bruises.

A few months later he sent me another email saying the band had just returned from playing a show at the Mercury Lounge in the lower East Side in New York and another show in Toronto. While there they had visited Niagara Falls. He was now looking forward to recuperating in Sheffield for a few weeks before heading back out on the road for the next tour.

After that, I didn't receive any further emails. The group managed to release one more album, *Seven Miles of Love* (2004), before splitting soon after. And though they toured heavily while they were together, the group never seemed make it to the next level. But then again, with the kind of fast rock and roll lifestyle they were practicing, it wouldn't have helped in giving the group stamina and longevity in a highly competitive and tough industry. Eventually the lifestyle will catch up with you.

Looking back on the album's recording sessions twenty years later in 2023 Colin Elliot, who co-produced three of the tracks on the album with Richard Hawley, recalled a band who were firing on all cylinders.

"On the drums, Richie was such a hard hitter and a really

solid player," Elliot affirmed. "And I really loved Bailey's bass playing. I mean, he was kind of a one string Rickenbacker, all down strokes on the plectrum, but superb." Elliot was surprised the band never reached their potential and believes inner band tensions eventually caused the band to implode. "I still don't know why they split but I think they eventually fell out. Hugh had a few issues, and Tom was maybe pushing the band a certain way, so they weren't getting on quite so well anymore."

In the aftermath Smith relocated to Edinburgh for a time before returning to Sheffield and to his previous occupation of chef, while Hogg and Bailey went on to form The Hosts and Westley joined Reverend and the Makers. Bailey also relocated to Barcelona where he ran a vintage clothes business.

****

Swedish-American outfit Carolina Liar were a classic case of industry hype and how, the faster things move, the faster they also burn. Having signed to a major label in 2008 and released a modestly successful debut album, by the time of their second album's release in 2011 the band had returned to independent status after a dispute over the direction of their creative vision saw their departure from Atlantic Records. The rapid ascent of the band can also be measured by how quickly things were moving for the band at the time during their brief visit to Australia.

In September 2008 Carolina Liar principal songwriter and lead vocalist Chad Wolf and guitarist Jim Almgren Gândara were in Melbourne for a quick two-day promo visit to capitalize on their recently released debut album *Coming to Terms* which Warner Music Australia were hyping. To my ears the album sounded like a cross between The Killers and U2 in differing degrees, with lots of melodic electro-pop elements that are part and parcel of producer Max Martin's musical template, something which was to my musical taste.

My interview with the band was on a Friday very late in the afternoon and the pair had only arrived in the country about forty-eight hours earlier, their flight touching down at midnight and then they had to be up and ready for their first Australian television appearance at 6 am that same morning! They had pre-recorded an acoustic performance of their current single 'I'm Not Over' on Network Ten's popular *Morning Show* program which aired the morning of my interview with the band.

I was instructed to meet the pair at an inner suburban luxury hotel which sat on the banks of the Yarra River, a few kilometres from Melbourne's busy city centre around 5:30 pm. Being a Friday, the lobby was filled with many corporate workers enjoying an after-work drink and unwinding from a week at the office. Entertaining the punters and providing some soothing acoustic cover tunes to ease the weekend in was a solo artist set up in the corner of the hotel but who was being drowned out by the noise of the punters talking among themselves.

Upon my arrival, the pair were nowhere to be seen, so checking the details of the interview, and confirming that I was indeed at the right location, I put in a quick call to the label's publicist to discover their whereabouts, to be told that the pair were doing a live radio interview and would be running late for our interview. They finally surfaced an hour later accompanied by their tour manager and two record label personnel. They apologized for their lateness, and were in high spirits, with no visible signs of fatigue after a long day of promotional activities. Wolf stood out with his short stature and very friendly nature which was infectious. He was certainly relishing being in the country for the first time.

Before the interview began, their label shared the news that the band's new single had been one of the most added tracks across radio that week which called for a celebratory drink. Finding a quiet space we took a seat to conduct the interview, the label representatives also joined us but remained in the background observing proceedings.

Wolf, wearing a scarf and with his blond hair up in a ponytail, was very much in charge of the interview though

Gândara offered up his responses as well. Wolf's journey to form Carolina Liar was quite interesting and was plotted through a series of chance events. Moving from his Charleston, South Carolina home to Los Angeles, the struggling musician refined his song-writing craft by undertaking an apprenticeship stint under famed superstar songwriter Diane Warren before a chance meeting at a Los Angeles hotel with über Swedish pop producer Max Martin, whose credits include everyone from Britney Spears to Backstreet Boys amongst others, who offered Wolf a free plane ticket to Sweden, finally set the stage for the formation of Carolina Liar.

Aside from discussing the band's back story and the new album, it was interesting to hear the sort of lengths their label's marketing department went to promote the band. One such example was the ingenious idea of manufacturing promotional stickers that boldly proclaimed, 'I'm a liar…Carolinaliar.com'. Wolf mentioned they were hoping to return to Australia for a proper concert tour early in the new year, but it never happened.

I was their last interview for the day and of the promo itinerary, and afterwards they planned to spend the rest of the evening savouring the delights of the city, before flying out of Australia the very next day to begin a two-month tour of the US. Gândara departed the band the following year and after the group released *Wild Blessed Freedom* in 2011, nothing more was heard from them, even though the band have never officially split, and Wolf continues to make music and work in the industry.

6: Rock Me Tonite

When MTV began their first-ever broadcast at the stroke of midnight on August 1, 1981, little did anyone realise the effect it would have on popular music in the long term, and the way music would be consumed in future. It was revolutionary and culturally seismic and its effect is still being felt more than forty years later. Two years prior, English new wave pop outfit The Buggles had a worldwide smash hit, 'Video Killed the Radio Star' which topped the charts in many countries such as Australia, the UK, Sweden, Japan and others, although in the US it only managed to climb to #40 on the Billboard Hot 100 chart.

The song was uncannily prophetic, envisaging a huge shift towards music videos just a few years later. The popularity of MTV would see the shift from the purely audio judgement of music to one where visuals became more important than the music. The popular artists of the day, such as Michael Jackson, would utilize the enormous potential of video to propel their careers, and in Jackson's case, to scale heights of pop stardom not witnessed before.

Before the arrival of MTV radio was king, but that changed almost overnight. In the early years of the station's existence videos tended to reflect what was popular on radio at the time, but that soon shifted as MTV became ever more popular and powerful in breaking new artists. Radio, which previously held sway, slowly lost its grip on listening audiences who turned to MTV for the latest sounds.

With the growth of the video industry, the corridors of power at the record labels suddenly allowed for lavish budgets so that their artists could feature in the most extravagant videos possible. This was done to capture the attention of music fans through the burgeoning medium of video, which in turn led to a surge in further album sales.

The video for Michael Jackson's 'Thriller' was 14 minutes long and was estimated to cost close to a million dollars, which for a music video was unprecedented at the time. But later that cost would become the norm and in some cases pale against videos later made by bands such as Duran Duran, whose 'Wild Boys' promo cost a cool million, or the video for Jackson's 1995 single 'Scream', which cost a staggering $7 million.

"MTV caused people to stop listening," confirms Billy Squier, who was one of the biggest rock acts in the world until a video for his 1984 song, 'Rock Me Tonite', which MTV aired in 'prime time', unceremoniously caused his career to nosedive virtually overnight. "Our musical heroes were now providing soundtracks for would-be film-directors who used our videos as stepping-stones to further their own careers, with little to no regard for the effect it might have on their clients."

Former Journey vocalist Steve Perry's video for his hit 1984 solo single 'Oh Sherrie', is a perfect example of how the video directors became the new platform for building their careers from music videos and underscores Squier's prescient observation. In "Oh Sherrie", Perry is resplendent in royal robes and crown, and as the strains of the song's synth intro chords begin, Perry suddenly stops, walks off set and tells the director, "This is ridiculous, I can't do this, this is not me."

I'll be delving into the whole 'Rock Me Tonite' saga in-depth later in this story but for now, while the damage done to Squier's career was significant, it paled in comparison to the carnage inflicted on music as an audio experience by the unintentional subjugation of rock radio and the elevation of style over substance via our TV screens. The ability for a listener to make a song their own, allowing them to create their own video in their mind, had been irretrievably lost.

****

Having first started out playing piano at the age of nine, before switching over to the guitar when he was thirteen, the American born Squier journeyed through a number of early bands through the late 1960s and into the 1970s, such as Kicks and The Sidewinders, before finally forming his own band, Piper, in 1976, in the role of principal songwriter, lead-vocalist and guitarist. The band would go on to ink a record deal with A&M Records, who released the group's eponymous debut in 1976 and follow-up *Can't Wait* in 1977. The group then hit the road opening for such acts as The Runaways and masked superstars KISS, before disbanding.

During his tenure with Piper, Squier's musical acumen and song-writing craftsmanship had been brought to the attention of Capitol Records, who signed him to a multi-album solo record deal in 1979, with his debut solo studio outing *The Tale of The Tape* appearing in the early months of 1980. The album showcased Squier's remarkable knack for writing catchy melodies and monstrous guitar riffs, something that would be refined to perfection on his second album, *Don't Say No*, issued the following year.

By the time of *Don't Say No*, Squier had made a quantum leap forward in both his musicianship and song-writing craft. An early indication of what would come to the fore on that album was quite noticeable when you take a listen two specific tracks by his band Piper: 'Whatcha Gonna Do' from Piper's first album and 'Drop by And Stay' from the second. Both clearly encompassed all that elements that would be given their fullest expression on *Don't Say No*.

"I had grown up on the Stones, The Beatles and The Who and that shaped my consciousness, though not in an overtly pop direction," says Squier. "The Stones were the edgiest part of that equation. It all started there before I quickly moved into Beck, Rod Stewart, Zeppelin, Jimi… where it started to get much edgier. I was of two minds, as I had great pop sensibilities and knew all about writing perfect three-minute songs, but found myself wanting to go for something that broke some boundaries, like the Stones did. When the Stones broke out in the sixties they were a blues-based band that also wrote a lot of consciously pop-oriented music. The Beatles, on the other hand, were a pop band who found themselves with a license to do whatever they wanted, and took the opportunity to expand on their original format. If you look at the Stones from the time they released *Beggar's Banquet*, through *Let It Bleed* and *Sticky Fingers* to *Exile on Main St…* those records came to define the Rolling Stones. Keith [Richards] and I have talked about that period, and we both agree, these are the records that capture the true essence of the band.

"Pete Townshend is a great pop songwriter who managed to branch out and start doing these extended musical jams that still revolved around the song, 'Won't Get Fooled Again' is a perfect example of Pete consolidating his position. And that's what I found myself going for, by the time I got to making *Don't Say No*. I had all these amazing influences I had grown up with and other new stuff I was really digging. And as I was playing in and out of bands and getting closer to becoming Billy Squier, I was always experimenting, trying to write different songs like that. I didn't know exactly where I wanted to go, but I was willing to travel."

Squier recalls the time whilst recording Piper's second album where he instinctively knew he had finally found his voice. One night, listening to a playback of the song 'Little Miss Intent', proved the turning point for Squier. "I had written that song right before we recorded the album," he says, "when I sang that song and heard it back in the studio, I felt like I was channelling Paul Rodgers. I thought, 'I'm there. I finally got it. I'm finally a singer'. It's not a direct comparison, but I thought, 'This is what he does, and I can do this too'. And though I was always pretty confident about my guitar-playing, my goal was never to go out and be a Hendrix or Page or Beck. My goal was to really learn from those guys and then take that knowledge and be able to transmit that into the songs that I was writing."

Squier had already clocked up more than ten years slogging

it out on the gigging circuit from his days in his early bands right through to Piper, all the while developing his song-writing craft, which was crystallized on *Don't Say No*. "My writing was always evolving," he says, "I wrote all the material for that album in two weeks, as I was really focused and wanted the record to be a concise representation of who Billy Squier was. I had worked to find my voice, so if I had something to say, it was going to be distinct and my own. I put words together to get people's attention, whether they fully understood them or not... I just did it. If you read through the lyrics, there's a style emerging, a certain uniqueness, stuff you may not have heard before. I threw everything I had at it. I wanted the lyrics to create pictures. Jim Steinman later commented, when we were working on *Signs of Life*, that my lyrics were very cinematic.

Don't Say No also set the template for Squier's signature hybrid of pop and rock influences that leaned more towards the heavier side of the rock spectrum. "Absolutely, without a doubt, I took all the lessons I learned from all the people who really meant a lot to me, the singers and musicians, and passed it all through the prism of my collected experience… and I just got it. It's a very significant and distinctive record from a song-writing standpoint. I found the balance that's made me great at what I do. Listen to the hooks: 'In the Dark', 'The Stroke', 'My Kinda Lover' — these are all 'hit' records. Then listen to 'Lonely Is the Night', 'Whadda You Want from Me', and 'Too Daze Gone' — you don't get a whole lot more rambunctious than that. I mixed it all together. That's probably what was unique about me, nobody had ever really quite done that. I had this great combination of influences and I just put 'em all together and said, why not?"

'The Stroke', released as the first single from the album in May 1981, solidified Squier's position in the lexicon of rock and roll history, beginning his ascendency to becoming one of the decade's biggest rock artists. Endless touring soon saw him move from opening act for bands such as Foreigner and Journey to headlining his own shows before the year ended. That same year also saw him embark on his first UK tour as support for Whitesnake in May and then a second jaunt in August, again as support for Whitesnake but also as one of the headline acts at the Reading Rock Festival. *Don't Say No* would be home to two more hit singles, 'In the Dark' and 'My Kinda Lover'.

As a teenager who had just picked up the guitar, the riff heavy tunes and melodies of *Don't Say No* really appealed to me. It rocked hard and it was loud, and those riffs and songs were so cool, they became part of my guitar learning regime. Also, the denim clad rocker's image also appealed to this fifteen-year-old pimply teenager too. Squier's music was my escape from the mundane outside world and into a world that spoke to me, and to who I was. He showed me, if I could play the guitar, I could aspire to be just like him, a rock star.

I first heard 'The Stroke' while listening to the *American Top 40* radio show hosted by Casey Kasem. I would tune in on my shortwave radio to the show, as a lot of the times a new release would first be issued or make the charts in the United States before they began appearing on Australian radio playlists. 'The Stroke' wouldn't see release in Australia until July 1981, two months after it's American release.

Squier appeared on an episode of Australia's popular television music show, *Countdown*, in late 1981 as part of a promotional visit for the album. He had come over just for a quick four-day visit as he was in the middle of a US tour with Foreigner. Dressed casually in jeans and sneakers and sitting opposite the show's host, Ian 'Molly' Meldrum, who started the interview by mentioning how there was a heavy-metal resurgence happening and then proceeded to ask Squier, "Do you like being labelled heavy-metal?" When I saw that interview, I couldn't believe it. What an embarrassing and uninformed question. Had Meldrum even listened to the album? The look on Squier's face revealed a sense of bewilderment as he curtly replied, "it's a little misleading, as my music is much broader than that term would imply."

After the interview, Meldrum asked Squier when

Australians would be able to see him tour the country to which Squier said that he was hoping to tour Australia the following year. Unfortunately that never happened and Squier — to the disappointment of his Aussie fans — never set foot on our shores.

At the tail end of 1981, 'Christmas Is the Time to Say "I Love You"' b/w 'White Christmas' was issued in time for the holiday season and went on to become a favourite of MTV — it was the first video filmed live in the MTV studios — that saw Squier performing the song and being joined by the MTV hosts. Squier's third album, *Emotions in Motion*, followed in 1982, and with a cover designed by pop art pioneer Andy Warhol, it again further propelled Squier's upward trajectory, with the album becoming his second US Top 5 entry and also going multi-platinum. Like *Don't Say No*, it was co-produced by Reinhold Mack, better known for his production work with Queen — in fact, Freddie Mercury and Roger Taylor would guest on backing vocals on the title track but the final sessions were marred by creative differences between Mack and Squier, which led Squier to remix the album to his liking, despite protestations from Mack. Squier and Mack would also team up to contribute the track, 'Fast Times (The Best Years of Our Lives)' to the soundtrack of the 1982 film, *Fast Times at Ridgemont High* which starred Sean Penn and Jennifer Jason Leigh.

Now a headlining act himself, and having just completed a huge sell-out tour, Squier tapped producer Robert 'Mutt' Lange for what would become Squier's fourth album, 1984's *Signs of Life*, but with Lange under pressure to finish The Cars *Heartbreak City* album and the sessions running overtime, Lange cited personal grievances for backing away from the project on the eve of the recording. Jim Steinman was subsequently enlisted as co-producer alongside Squier, and with Steinman's influence the album saw a more keyboard-tinged outing, making it even more palatable for radio, something which would be underscored by the commercial success of the album's lead single, 'Rock Me Tonite', which garnered Squier his highest charting single to date. Queen's Brian May would also make a guest appearance contributing a guitar solo on the track, '(Another) 1984'.

Around this time Squier also contributed a track called 'On Your Own' to the soundtrack album of Giorgio Moroder's restored and new edit of the classic 1927 silent movie *Metropolis*. He would repeat the process the following year by contributing 'Shake Down' to another film soundtrack album for *St. Elmo's Fire*.

With the *Signs of Life* album in the can and readied for release, and with video now becoming an essential part of a release package so the mighty powers-that-be at MTV could add it to their playlist, plans were afoot to produce an official video for the album's lead single, 'Rock Me Tonite'. Previously, Squier's videos had featured live performance-styled footage, showing Billy doing what he did best, performing to fans with his band, showing off his highly animated stage moves, all the while singing and bashing his guitar without missing a beat. For 'Rock Me Tonite', it was decided that it would feature more of a story line and MTV would be granted the 'world première' rights. Bob Giraldi, who had written and directed Michael Jackson's 'Beat It' video the year prior, was lined up to shoot it, but at the last minute Giraldi had misgivings about how his children might perceive the video and backed out.

"So now we have to get someone else," explains Squier today. "So, we took a meeting with an English director named David Mallet, who was very well thought of at the time, and he did some storyboards for me. The next thing I saw, I was riding into a diner on a white horse. And so, he was gone too. Now it's a month before the record's coming out and Capitol Records has given MTV the world première, so the schedule's locked in, and we've still got to shoot a video. So my girlfriend at the time (Australian costume-designer Fleur Thiemeyer) brings to my attention a very well-known choreographer, Kenny Ortega. She told me that Kenny really wanted to direct the project, and that he had an idea, and 'Could he talk to you about it?' And I said, 'OK, yeah…let's talk'.

"He was a great choreographer who'd been doing Michael Jackson and all sorts of noteworthy performers. So, he came to me, and we talked, and it was his idea to do a performance video of what I'm used to doing on stage. He also happened to be gay and had never directed a video, but was very keen, and had an interesting idea to shoot me without the band and script my various stage-moves — which he'd seen in my live shows — to the music. As I'm always looking for a new challenge, I liked the concept. I had no concerns as to how it might be interpreted and I have nothing against gay people, I want to be very clear about that. I thought, 'What a great idea. It's not a story that has no relation to the song. It's me, it's a performance where we choreograph what I do on stage, then bring the band in at the end.' I really liked the idea — it was different but didn't really deviate from the basics of my performances. Everyone said 'OK, let's go'. And that's when the trouble started."

Ortega — later to find fame as director of the *High School Musical* franchise — wanted the video to feature a scene that recalled Tom Cruise dancing across the room in his underwear playing air guitar in the film *Risky Business*. Squier was adamant he did not want that and instructed Ortega to evoke the edginess and feel of the film *American Gigolo*: sultry, sinewy and in black and white.

"We had brought on a highly respected director of photography," explains Squier, "and I made myself very clear, 'It's not *Risky Business*, it's *American Gigolo*,' and the DP goes, 'fine'. And because we had all watched *American Gigolo*, I wasn't worried about where we're going. Then we get on the set, and I see the bed with satin sheets, and everything is colourful, pastel and poppy. And I went, 'What the fuck is this? This is not the idea.' And Kenny says, 'we have to do this, because when we use the smoke-machines and fog up the set and blah-blah-blah, then it will be what you want.'"

In one scene in the video, Squier can be seen crawling across the stage, looking up at the camera with a sort of come-hither look. In another, he changes into a pink top and then picks up a pink guitar. "I think in the end, Ortega got what he wanted," says Squier. "But he didn't give me what I needed and that's on him; he maintains to this day that he only did what I told him to do, that I was totally in charge of everything that went down. His word against mine, but I can tell you, that is a complete lie... a complete lie.

"You have to believe these guys — it's what they do — it's not what I do. But when I saw the cut in the editing-room, it didn't look any different than when we were on the set, and I was absolutely horrified. What I saw was a video that did not connect with who I was on stage. Kenny put in a few questionable moves that he wanted me to do, and I trusted him because it was his concept and he'd seen me perform — I thought that he really knew what I was about and respected me, but he didn't. He had his own ideas of who Billy Squier should be. I didn't want it to come out, but I had no support."

At this point in his career Squier was one of the biggest artists in America, and his label Capitol Records had promised MTV a world première, which to them seemed like a great coup at the time. So, to placate Squier's ever growing concerns about the video, they reassured Squier that he needn't worry about the video, as the song was a smash hit.

"The label came down to the editing-room in Los Angeles, along with one of my managers," recalls Squier. "They didn't say this to me directly, but it's clear Capitol didn't want to not give MTV this video. We could have pulled it and said, 'We'll come back with something else.' But I think that they just didn't want to go there. They didn't want to upset their relationship with MTV. Why? Because MTV was now the biggest 'radio station' in the country. MTV had usurped radio.

"I remember standing at the console watching this disaster, and I just wanted to kill this guy who had sold me out for his own little wet dream of a video. My main manager at the time had decamped to England to be with his mother, who was having some health problems, and he'd had gone back to look after her, which is understandable. But he took himself completely out of the picture and left me with no one who was really in a position to stand up to the label and force a tough decision. So, there we were, and management basically acquiesced and went along with the label's position. Instead of saying, 'No, this isn't coming out', what I got was, 'Yeah, it should be okay.'"

With the première looming and an upcoming tour scheduled, Squier and Thiemeyer left the screening-room and headed to the airport, as they had planned a bit of time away in Europe before the tour kicked off. In the car Thiemeyer — who, let's not forget, had started this whole mess — turned to Squier and said, "You're fucked!"

No one could have foreseen the effect the video would have on Squier's career. In the aftermath of the video's broadcast, Squier saw his audience dwindle almost immediately overnight. Prior to the video he had been playing to full arenas, but once the video hit the television screens, he began playing to half-filled ones.

To paraphrase Ray Davies of The Kinks, how could four minutes of 'celluloid' provoke such a controversy, when at the same time you had Mick Jagger and David Bowie prancing down the street, singing on Broadway and kissing each other? And forty years after the video, many questions still remain unanswered

In the 2011 book, *I Want My MTV: The Uncensored Story of the Music Video Revolution* by Craig Marks and Rob Tannenbaum, a chapter titled, 'A Whopping, Steaming Turd' is dedicated to the 'Rock Me Tonite' video which the book ranked as the worst video ever made. Some of Squier's contemporaries chime in with their thoughts, all agreeing with the worst video accolade. What's ironic to me though, are comments from musicians such as Def Leppard's Phil Collen who states in the book, "…singers shouldn't skip through their bedroom, ripping their shirts off." And this from a guy who has become synonymous with taking his shirt off and performing shirtless on stage! Collen's comment is both laughable and hypocritical.

Looking back forty years later Mark Goodman, one of the MTV VJs at the time of the video's broadcast told me, "I have no idea why that particular video got people in such a tizzy! There are plenty of bad videos to choose from that were not career-enders! I don't have much of a recollection of anyone being any more bent out of shape about this video than any other classically bad video. 'Separate Ways' from Journey is worse in my view."

****

As a teenager the video never bothered me — in fact, the first thought that came to my mind was that Squier's female fan base would find it very appealing. What I find laughable today and in hindsight is that just a few short years later, Sunset Strip would be teeming with hair-metal bands pushing effeminacy to the utmost degree: makeup, big hair, lipstick, colourful clothes and pink guitars! The late eighties guitar-shredders were the champions of pink guitars, colours that were much sought after in their arsenal of six strings. Yet none of them suffered any damage to their careers, in fact the whole Sunset Strip scene took over the musical and visual landscape for a number of years before the arrival of grunge in the early nineties brought it to an abrupt end. Goodman agrees. "Billy's colour scheme and his moves aside, you can also point out glam metal as it was already happening and was going strong at that point. [Bands such as] Ratt, Twisted Sister and WASP were all doing something like that. Not to mention before them Bowie, T-Rex, Mick Jagger etc."

Jay Sosnicki, actor, and punk-rock singer (aka Zsa) from L.A. band The Cocks and long-time Squier fan agrees, "for the record, I think the whole 'the "Rock Me Tonite" video ruined his career' thing is somewhat apocryphal and has only grown as the years have gone by. If you look at his earlier videos, he always flounced around like that, just less so. My less-enlightened buddies questioned his sexuality long before

'Rock Me Tonite' — I just think that with 'Rock Me Tonite' he took his very unique, slightly goofy dance style to its extreme. That, combined with crawling on the ground like Madonna, the onanistic mirror stuff and the ripping off his own tee-shirt as if he couldn't stand to not pay tribute to his own unbelievable hotness is what did that video in. As with much of eighties pop culture, it was just over-the-top and unintentionally funny. We all make mistakes."

My personal view is that, taken everything into context, Squier was subconsciously tapping into the zeitgeist of what was to come, in particular the changing cultural landscape, as the AIDS epidemic was just starting to make its mark on society, causing fear and ignorance to ripen… a scenario best exemplified by the controversy which surrounded Queen's video for 'I Want to Break Free' that came out a few short months before Squier's video. In that video Queen parade around in drag in a mock send-up of long-running British television soap opera *Coronation Street* and, while outside of America most people got the joke, when it came to US audiences, the humour of the video along with the meaning of the song's subject matter got lost in translation.

Instead, the cross dressing and Mercury's overt gay overtones proved distasteful to middle America and more especially MTV who, already wielding much power, gave it as little airing as possible, which in turn didn't help the single climb much higher than #45 on the US chart. Intrinsically the ensuing saga shone a light on the underlining homophobia that was running rampant at the time. Ironically, for those outside America, and who understood the significance of the subject matter in the song, it became the go-to anthem for freedom from oppression, and the freedom to be oneself!

"America was extremely homophobic in the early 80s… not that it ever came up on my radar," says Squier. "I'd had gay friends and associates since the day I wandered into the music business. I'd also been schooled on artists who made sexual ambiguity a component of their personas. But girls were always 'it' for me, so I never gave it much thought. One thing I witnessed when I toured with my friends Queen on their *Hot Space/Emotions* US tour in 1982. Freddie had premièred his new look — short hair, moustache, tank top and audiences weren't too keen on it. Queen left town and didn't come back to America again until 2006, with Paul Rodgers on vocals. When Freddie put that image in front of American audiences, their love-affair with America was over.

"My female fans had no issue with the video at all, but I lost a big part of my hard-core male audience. If you were a big Billy Squier fan, you knew Billy Squier as a guitar-slinger who came out on stage and just tore it up; sweat and virility prowling the stage. But then all of sudden that video came out and makes you think that he is not the person you thought he was, there's another side he's showing you: a little more androgynous and playing a pink guitar, frolicking on satin sheets and you start to question why? If you're a girl, that might not bother you too much, you might even dig it. But if you're a guy, and now you say, 'I love Billy Squier', well, does that make you gay?

"Homophobia was hotting up in 1984. I became a subconscious threat to their manhood, because they now see this guy who they viewed as a one-man Led Zeppelin suddenly become, I don't know what, but it wasn't that. And I think that's what caused the backlash."

"People sometimes forget that Queen was never a thing in America until *Wayne's World,*" explains Sosnicki. "And certainly, every move Freddie Mercury made onstage, especially after adopting his '70s Castro "clone" look, telegraphed loud and clear what terrified straight boys suspected. Rob Halford is another example, certainly with the way he presented onstage in Judas Priest with the bondage clothes and his cat-like saunter, gay rumours abounded. Yet Priest were huge with the generally homophobic heavy metal audience of the time despite this. Which suggests that Billy's sudden fall from grace was less about the 'Rock Me Tonite' video than the possibility that he might simply have been out of big hit songs."

Mitch Davis, a respected New York producer and musician who later collaborated with Squier, disagrees with Sosnicki's hypothesis that Squier may have been out of hit songs. "I don't think it's because of the songs themselves or the overall image for the album or the other videos," he says. "I love that album. It's what I'd expect from a Billy Squier album. The song did great on the charts and people loved it, but then at some point, people started talking about the video. That kind of stuff happens all the time, someone makes an observation about an otherwise innocuous thing and then everyone is like 'oh, yeah, THAT!'"

As far as Sosnicki is concerned, he never questioned whether Squier was straight, it never set off alarm bells for him, the same way that Mercury and Halford did. "I think I can explain his appeal to gay men vis-a-vis 'Rock Me Tonight', and why it made straight guys so uncomfortable," he states categorically. "The song itself was a pretty blunt call for sex — "rock" standing in euphemistically for a more direct verb — which tracks for the promiscuity of the 80s generally, and for pre-AIDS gay culture specifically. But more importantly, I think the video's appeal had more to do with its relation to the freedom of the dance floor which, for gay men of that era, cannot be underestimated. It was one of the few places where we could fully express ourselves without censure. And I think the over-the-top way Squier presents in the video — his unabashed and narcissistic celebration of his own beauty and physicality, resonated for a lot of gay men because it reflected those dance floor moments of self- expression. Here it is. Take it or leave it. That's pretty powerful. It's also the thing that made straight guys squirrelly. He was being himself without shame in a private moment that the world was allowed to see. Without worrying about how a guy is supposed to dance or look, or be."

"I didn't pay attention to that video other than... it was a rock and roll video," remembers Grammy award-winning producer and guitarist Larry Mitchell who was the touring guitarist for Squier on his *Creatures of Habit* tour. "It wasn't until

I got on a tour that people suddenly were saying, 'you should check out that video'. I think the first couple of times people said it to me, I didn't quite understand what they were talking about. They were like, 'yeah, the video that ruined his career'. And I'm like, what? But I didn't pay attention to it until then. I don't remember thinking it was a great video or a bad video or anything of it, other than, it was a good song."

The backlash to the 'Rock Me Tonite' video confirmed just how big MTV had become and how the visual medium became the driving force of the music industry. The music took a back seat. It didn't matter how good or bad the music was, if the video imagery was appealing and popular, it would sell the music. I always wondered over the years, if Billy had included a scantily clad nubile young lady in the video, whether it would have received the same kind of reaction. The hair-metal bands went to market when it came to featuring big hair, high-heeled, lingerie-wearing young women in their videos.

"The 80s were all about guy bands that looked like they had better hair than their girlfriends, used more hairspray than the girls in the audience and wore tighter pants," concurs Mitchell. "I remember bands going on stage who had actually borrowed clothes from their girlfriends!"

Who can ever forget the imagery of the cartwheeling antics of Tawny Kitaen in Whitesnake's 'Here I Go Again' video or Van Halen's 'Hot for Teacher', where a pair of school teachers underdress down to their bikinis in front of their young class? Maybe including something like that would have changed the trajectory of Billy's career? We will never know. Regardless, there was more going on behind the scenes than what was in clear view. I wholeheartedly don't for a minute accept that what occurred to Billy in the wake of the 'Rock Me Tonite' video was primarily down to the video alone, too many other elements come into play and need to be considered. As mentioned, you had AIDS and homophobia running rampant. Add to this, Squier's own admission that he sought to be in control of his creative output, especially in the studio, where his musical vision was to be fully expressed as he saw fit and not diluted by outside hands, which caused him to be incorrectly labelled by some as a 'control freak'. And Squier's integrity didn't help matters in an industry where loyalty and integrity are not prioritized.

With the release of 'Rock Me Tonite', having lost all say in how his image was to be projected, and with no support from management and his label in getting the video pulled, he found that friends had turned to foes. From supporters to non-supporters.

"Everyone was quick to cover their asses," confirms Squier, "and all the finger-pointing was directed at me. My 'manager-in absentia' put forth the misplaced notion that the record wasn't a success — not because of the video, but because the songs weren't good enough. Sounds like he wanted to deflect attention from the video, rather than accept his partial culpability for what happened. He wasn't there to defend his biggest client; he didn't stand up for me. So he shrugged it off, 'Oh, the songs weren't good enough'. Well, that's bullshit. I didn't leave the business for nine years after that, but I started to look at things a lot differently from this point on.

"Everything that came after that was a little bit more insidious and not quite as dramatic. But more and more people were making an art out of self-serving, dishonest behaviour, and you constantly had to watch your back, because they were climbing the ladder at your expense, following wherever the current trend led them."

Davis laughs at any suggestion that all those working for the artist would know what's best for the artist. "I don't think managers know more about an artist's audience than the artist himself," he says. "They don't necessarily know who's in touch with what. To tell an artist, 'You need this producer coming in to do this' is not what it's about for an artist like Billy where they created who they are. The artist knows what they're doing and they know their sound. To say you're not in touch with a modern audience is really saying then that, the label doesn't get the artist. People like an artist because of what the artist does.

And I think the audiences grow with the artists, too. You make music for yourself, and if you're lucky, there's an audience who is right there with you. They're along for that ride and if you suddenly change what you're doing to somehow target them better, then it's changing what the fans originally signed up for.

"Especially with someone like Billy, who has such a unique and definable sound… it's impossible to say he was not in touch with X because he never was X in the first place. He was successful because he did his own thing. All I can say is that I think those songs are great songs and I know that I did not, nor did any of my friends, think anything of it. He was just as he always was."

What drove Squier to exit the music industry nine years later would only confirm, without a doubt, that all the elements mentioned above were indeed at play. In 1993, newly appointed Capitol Records boss Gary Gersh told Squier he believed Squier's newly recorded album, *Tell the Truth*, was the best album Capitol would release in the upcoming year, but then openly told him he would bury the album.* For Squier, that became the straw that finally broke the camel's back, and he made his decision to leave the industry.

Squier believes MTV marked the beginning of the change in music, with the days of being an artist finally over, something he foreshadowed back in 1981 with 'The Stroke'. "MTV didn't kill the music on purpose," he says, "but they robbed listeners of that special communion between an individual's imagination and a voice on the radio. Songs became soundtracks for would-be film directors show-reels. That's when it started. You could plot it on a graph: 1981 was the beginning of the end for rock as we knew it."

****

---

* "Billy Squier Recalls the Label Woes That Ended His Recording Career" Giles, Jeff. May 30, 2014; https://ultimateclassicrock.com/billy-squier-tell-the-truth/

Another example of the might of MTV's visual power to influence and reshape the music-loving masses is confirmed by Mark King from 1980s English jazz-funk-popsters Level 42. "What a music video did for your career being played on MTV was enormous," King told me. "It meant that they could be playing your song even while you were on tour in Japan or in Germany or some place on the planet, as your song and your image would be up there on the screen. And the initial start of all of that was, for example, *Brothers in Arms* the Dire Straits album and all of that incredible stuff, Aha's 'Take on Me' where they were starting to use like cartoon stuff which then turned into real people and, you know Duran Duran's 'Rio', where they're on this yacht and they're selling this whole aspirational dream, and those Prince videos, all of this stuff was an incredible tool.

"I found it interesting. I was trying to have some kind of input as to what was going to happen to us. Consequently, you got videos from us like 'Something About You' (1985) which basically was centred around a sort of clown image. I just happen to have seen a film called *The Entertainer*, which featured this character Archie Rice, who was played by Laurence Olivier, who was this sort of manic-depressive comedian working on the South Coast in the UK back in the musical-hall days and he was just putting on this facade all the time. It had nothing to do with the song, it was just a character that I thought might be quite cool to have in the video. And the Americans absolutely loved that idea so much so that when we made the follow up video for the next single, 'Leaving Me Now' (1985), we didn't have that character planned to be in it at all but the Americans came straight on and said, 'well, where's the clown character? You need to have that in this next video too as you need some kind of consistency in this'. And that sort of spoke volumes really for how they saw it and how we used it."

Squier rode out the controversy of 'Rock Me Tonite' by first firing his management team and then spending the rest of 1984 on the road in support of *Signs of Life*, with glam-metal group Ratt as support for the majority of the tour dates, before Southern rockers Molly Hatchet joined him for a few remaining dates at the tail end of the tour. Squier would not tour again until 1989. In hindsight, *Signs of Life's* synth-layered textures meshed to Squier's guitar framework were perfectly matched without losing any of Squier's heavy duty guitar riffage and melodicism, and *Signs of Life* very much shows Squier is at the pinnacle of his career.

The album overall is a solid outing and very consistent, and in the aftermath of the drama that unfolded with 'Rock Me Tonite', a follow-up single 'All Night Long' was issued as the album's second official single, though it only managed to reach #75 on the US chart. I particularly like the Peter Gunn-esque 'Eye on You', the gritty 'Take A Look Behind Ya', the galloping '(Another) 1984' and 'Reach for The Sky' (later the title would be used by glam-metal group RATT for their 1988 album) which echoed a Moody Blues vibe along with a blistering '80s flashy styled guitar solo.

Yet there is one track that tends to get overlooked, 'Fall for Love' which, for me, is an underrated slow burn of a song. I can't understand why critics have continually lambasted this track over the years, maybe it's because of Squier's more spoken type vocals in the verses, or maybe they have never given the track time to allow it to grip their ears fully… whatever they think, I personally consider it a brilliant track, and one that oozes with a new wave-ish spirit, and a hooky refrain that shows Squier was not afraid to detour down the road less travelled. And the very arty cover design by famed cover art designer Bill Smith, who had done covers for artists such as The Rolling Stones and Queen to name but a few, was uniquely cool, too.

****

Squier spent the beginning of 1985 in Nepal, before coming home to write his next album. Though he had enjoyed working with Steinman, Squier was advised by his label and new management that he was losing touch with the times and needed a more contemporary producer. At the same time, Squier also renegotiated the largest recording-contract in the industry, which tied him to Capitol for another seven years.

With English producer Peter Collins at the helm, Squier entered the studio to begin pre-production on what would become his fifth album, *Enough Is Enough*. Alternating between the Power Station in New York and Sarm East in London, recording sessions were again fraught with difficulty, with Squier and Collins at loggerheads when it came to their respective methods of working and vision. Squier again felt increasingly isolated by his support team, with the album's title perfectly summing up his frustration. The finished result wasn't to Squier's liking so, after firing Collins, he returned to the studio and salvaged the recording as best he could, though full production credit was still given to Collins.

Enough Is Enough finally appeared in September 1986, and 'Love Is the Hero' was issued as the lead single from the album. It featured an inspired vocal performance from Freddie Mercury — still one of the biggest superstars in the rock world [outside of America] — but only managed to reach #80 on the Billboard Hot 100. Mercury also featured on the track 'Lady with a Tenor Sax', as co-writer with Squier. A video showcasing Squier and Mercury wasn't even contemplated by the label.

By this time the enormous pull and might of MTV saw it become a monolith, diversifying and extending into additional specialty shows such as *Headbangers Ball* to cater for the ever-growing popularity of heavy metal, and *Yo! MTV Raps*, for the burgeoning hip-hop scene, and with its emphasis on the visual sound-tracked by music, it influenced the film industry, where carefully curated music took a much more prominent positioning in films, and another vehicle for increased record sales.

It would be nearly three years before Squier released his next studio outing, 1989's *Hear & Now*, which recaptured more of the harder-edge rock sound of *Don't Say No*. Though it was a fine return to form for Squier, sales were nowhere near what they were at his early eighties commercial peak. But regardless of how good the music — or how bad — artists' popularity was now being driven completely by MTV. The bigger and more visual the video, the more rotation and eventual surge in sales. Some of the year's biggest selling albums were driven primarily by their videos.

After a few years in the MTV wilderness, Squier was finally back on screen and in rotation with his performance-styled video for the album's lead single, 'Don't Say You Love Me'. Directed by Andy Morahan (who also directed George Michael's video for 'Faith'), it was sprinkled with cameos of alluring women in various stages of attire dancing in the rain. Squier also returned to the road for a bout of touring in support of the album.

Squier's next album, 1991's *Creatures of Habit*, though a strong and solid outing, found itself lost amongst the then rising popularity of grunge and alternative rock, which would completely overhaul the musical landscape and end the reign of most of the eighties' rockers and the entire hair-metal brigade. The shift from the most colourful and outlandish to a more earthy, minimalistic charity-shop look also infiltrated every MTV video. Again, as it did withthe fashions and sounds of the eighties, MTV now adopted the same approach for New Kids on the Block to Nirvana's 'Smells Like Teen Spirit', aptly illustrated when MTV placed the video on heavy rotation, helping to usher in the grunge sounds of the 1990s.

Squier again hit the road to tour in support of the new album. "I had an absolutely great time on that *Creatures of Habit* tour," recalls Mitchell. "Though Billy always knew what he wanted, I don't remember not having any freedom. When I came to learning the songs, Billy made some suggestions here and there, but gave me space to do solos and stuff. I knew Billy was a really good rhythm player, as his timing, feel and groove were great. But I didn't know how good of a lead player he was as well until we actually got in the rehearsal room. I had no idea, so I wasn't prepared for that. He was absolutely a great lead player too."

Creatures Of Habit would also mark the final time Squier would make an appearance on the music charts. Two years later and seven years after the 'Rock Me Tonite' controversy, *Tell the Truth*, Squier's eighth album appeared in March of 1993 and was produced by Mike Chapman who told Squier, "You are the best songwriter I've ever worked with".

Former New York Dolls guitarist Steve Conte, who contributed guitar and backing vocals on several of the album's tracks, concurs with Chapman's statement. "It's really a shame what happened to this album as the whole thing really stands the test of time," he says. "Billy sings his ass off on it! And Billy was great about letting me do my thing, though if he heard something he didn't like or heard differently he would step in. Luckily there wasn't too much if any of that happening with my guitar parts. In fact, there were some things that I wasn't sure I liked that he liked — so who was I to insist I change it? It's his album after all, and it's a really great one."

Squier and Chapman both believed it was his best album to date, but on the eve of the album release, tensions were running high. The single released from the album, 'Angry' encapsulated Squier's feelings about what he had endured from the industry and prophetically foretold what was to come:

> *Wrapped my life in chains.*
> *Gave my everything.*
> *Learned to feel no pain.*
> *Now every day I wake up, Angry…*

Squier sings in the first verse clearly pissed off at his lot, before firing off with the one-two punch of…

> *I've wasted too much time.*
> *I'm gettin' down off the rack.*
> *I'm packin' up all my crimes*
> *And I ain't comin' back.*

When Gersh, who had just taken over as head of Capitol

Records, told Squier he was done, Squier immediately called his lawyer, and the Capitol Records era was over. Though still owing Capitol one more record as part of his contract, in the end it was a win for Squier, who secured the rights to his master recordings after Capitol agreed to buy him out of his contract. And then he walked away.

"*Tell The Truth* is one of his best, right up there with *Don't Say No,*" affirms Conte. "Yet it didn't get any promotion, videos, singles, or anything. The label just let it come out and die. Who could blame him for walking away from the biz? It's fucking heartbreaking to make a record that good, and then have an executive at your label tell you, 'I'm gonna make sure it fails!'"

While the 'Rock Me Tonite' video marked the point at which Squier's career curved, it certainly wasn't the culprit we've all been led to believe it was over all these decades. As already outlined, many other elements were at play and need to be considered. Clearly the power that was MTV, the lack of support from his record label, who consistently undermined Squier along with his management, and the cultural climate of the AIDS epidemic, all together played their role in bringing to pass Squier's downward career trajectory. And the responsibility lays at their feet.

As he adjusted to his new life away from the music business, he swapped his guitar for a pen and wrote his first original screenplay, *Run to Daylight,* which achieved a placing on the short-list of the 1994 Sundance Film Festival, though the screenplay never made it onto the screen. Four years later in 1998, a song Squier wrote in memory of his friendship with Freddie Mercury titled 'I Have Watched You Fly' was debuted in the theatrical performance of the monodrama, *Mercury: The Afterlife and Times of a Rock God.* The same year he issued, independently, the blues-soaked acoustic album *Happy Blue,* which, while a huge departure from the signature Squier musical template, showed him in a more introspective setting devoid of production gimmicks and over-kill.

Forty years later and looking back on that whole video

controversy and the aftermath that ensued, Squier asserts; "The video didn't kill me, but it hurt. It was hard at the time. But it didn't change who I was fundamentally. It wasn't a 'lights out' moment."

Conte agrees. "I don't think that video ended his career, as Billy went on to make a bunch more really good records after that," he says. "Everyone has probably got their own idea about that video. Billy had let his girlfriend at the time do the set design, the pink, the satin sheets and all of that. He was going a bit 'arty' with it and didn't mind letting out another side of him. I can totally relate to that kind of thing, having been in the New York Dolls of course, but then, they were known for that type of flamboyance. I guess Billy's main audience were like, hard rock dudes, Zeppelin-heads who didn't 'get it'. Billy told me the director had wanted a *Risky Business* dance scene kind of thing, and he got it."

Squier has struggled to understand the way that he and his video were singled out among the multitude of others that were way more controversial, and way more questionable, as with some of the aforementioned examples I've provided in this story. And when you consider for a moment that the roots of rock and roll music have always been about individuality and freedom, a mantra affirmed loud and clear by all who followed its path since its birth in 1950s — Little Richard and Elvis Presley being two who ignited outrage and controversy at the time — then watch a single video expressing those virtues wield the power over an artist's career, the subject becomes moot.

"I make a video, which to me is a visual addendum to the music and shouldn't even be important," he muses. "But I'm doing it because this is where the business is at, it's of utmost importance, and your record company wants you to do it. It's a new means of transporting your music to your audience. For me it was just a video, but what we got was the indictment of an artist. And that's never happened before. So how come I was denied that freedom? I didn't believe I was doing anything controversial. I never thought about that video having negative ramifications. It was an intriguing idea at the time, and I still think it was a good idea if Ortega hadn't gone off-script and crossed me the way he did.

"And all of that led me to this speculative conclusion. The scenario is that Billy Squier has just come out with two huge records in *Don't Say No* and *Emotions in Motion* back-to-back and he's either co-headlining with all the biggest bands in America or headlining himself. He's just done a huge tour of America too and helped break Def Leppard in the process. So, you look at that time in 1984, he's on the cusp. So, if *Signs of Life* comes out and does as well as *Emotions in Motion* and *Don't Say No*, or better, he is gold, forever. He would be firmly entrenched in the consciousness of at least American musical society. What if his male fans in this instance are more into him than he knows? Not in a sexual way, but I mean, if he is on the cusp of becoming a one man Led Zeppelin as they've labelled him and then the video comes out, and they see something which is not what they thought at all…?

"If I was an average artist in 1984, and I made a video like that, nobody would have noticed. People could have played it a little, maybe they wouldn't, maybe they just go, 'it sucks, we don't need it'. But nobody would have said anything. It just would have gone away. You see videos where people make fools of themselves all the time, and no one pays any mind.

"MTV didn't pick me, it was not their fault, they were just the vehicle. They didn't do it. So where does the reaction come from? Maybe I was a lot bigger than I thought. Maybe my fans had developed a very strong image of me, but all of a sudden, because of the video, that image was called into question."

Twenty-five years after his last release Squier issued the track, 'Harder on a Woman' in early 2023. A gritty foot-stomper driven by a blues-infused guitar riff, it has all the usual Squier hallmarks. The seeds for the song's genesis were first sown a decade earlier when Squier undertook writing sessions with swampy American blues musician C.C. Adcock. With Squier supplying vocals and guitar, he's helped by Simon Kirke, of

Free and Bad Company fame, on drums, guitar/wingman G.E. Smith, and long-time bassist Mark Clarke, who first played with Billy on *Don't Say No*.

Squier is currently one of the most widely-sampled artists in hip-hop, with the drum beat from his song 'The Big Beat' off his 1980 album *Tale of the Tape*, sampled by numerous acts from Britney Spears and Alicia Keys to Jay Z and Run DMC, to name just a few. 'The Stroke' has also been sampled many times, most notably by Eminem (Berserk) and Grandwizzard Johnny 'O and The Mighty Sorcerer Crew.

"I think in Billy's case, he was always a unique artist, which is why I think even now his stuff doesn't sound dated," confirms Davis, "most people who were big in the eighties, their stuff often sounds like it doesn't hold up. It has a very eighties production or eighties sound. But Billy's stuff, sounded like Billy's sound. It wasn't eighties music. It was Billy Squier music and that's why when you listen to it today it still sounds great. It sounds like him."

7: Mamma Mia

Sweden has always held a strong fascination for me ever since I first heard the sweet sounds of ABBA when I was ten years old. Back then ABBA and car manufacturer Volvo were two of the most widely known exports to come out of Sweden, though over the years the Nordic country would also give the world furniture giant IKEA and audio streaming titan Spotify amongst others.

Back in the mid-seventies Australia was gripped by ABBA mania. You could not get away from hearing an ABBA song on radio, and they were heavily featured on national music television show *Countdown*. And, in the wake of their enormous popularity, the doors opened for other Swedish musical exports to follow in their footsteps in the hope of achieving recognition and commercial success in Australia. Prior to their breakthrough, Australians had gotten a taste of what Sweden had to offer musically via Swedish group Blue Swede who scored an Australian Top 5 hit with 'Hooked on a Feeling' and instrumental combo The Spotnicks who had found favour with the instrumental music loving fraternity in the sixties.

Yet 1975 was the year that ABBA invaded Australia after *Countdown* aired videos for 'Mamma Mia' and 'I Do, I Do, I Do, I Do, I Do'. The visual aspect and the sweet pop sounds of the group instantly connected with not only the music-loving youth of the country, but people of all ages. And, though the group were at that point having success both in Sweden and Europe, the fame and fortune ABBA achieved in Australia helped pave the way for them to finally breakthrough on a worldwide scale. Mind you, at the time of ABBA's Australian breakthrough, they were competing with 'Rollermania' as tartan sensations Bay City Rollers scored hit after hit. Yet while the Roller hysteria would subside by 1977, ABBA would only get bigger and their Australian success would continue for several more years.

I bought ABBA's eponymous third album upon release and it became a much-played record in our household. I couldn't get the songs out of my head; they were earworms — the sugary sweet melodies, the wall of sound, those amazing vocals by the stunning Agnetha and Frida, and keyboard playing brilliance of Benny and Björn's star-shaped guitar, they had it all. And of course, their song-writing craft.

I consider this album the template that defined who ABBA were musically. Having already released two albums, and having their reputation based on their Eurovision win, at this point in their career they needed to prove themselves as credible music artists in their own right, and this album solidified their standing — the pop world would never be the same again.

Recording sessions ran between August 1974 and March 1975 through a succession of studios: Glenstudio, Stocksund and Metronome Studio in Stockholm, with the album finally seeing release in April 1975. Prior to the album's release two tracks were issued as singles in Australia: 'So Long' and 'I've Been Waiting for You', but it was the third single 'I Do, I Do, Do, I Do, I Do', that would take them to the top of the Australian charts for the first time and begin their reign as pop king and queens. Their follow-up singles from the same album, 'SOS' and 'Mamma Mia', would also go to number one.

A man who I would later come to know and record with, Janne Schaffer, played guitar on 'Mamma Mia', 'Hey, Hey Helen', 'SOS', 'Man in the Middle', 'Bang-A-Boomerang', 'So Long' and 'I've Been Waiting for You'. I loved how the group incorporated varying musical styles into the signature sound, from the infusion of glam rock and funk on 'Hey, Hey Helen' to the reggae rhythms of 'Tropical Loveland' to the sax-driven 1950s-esque orchestral sounds of 'I Do, I Do, I Do, I Do, I Do'.

"ABBA were like The Beatles," according to Mike Watson, who, along with Rutger Gunnarsson, shared bass playing duties on all the ABBA albums. "They did everything from a music hall kind of thing to rock and roll. They were all very unique songs." Watson, who also famously portrayed Napoleon on the cover of ABBA's 1974 album, *Waterloo*, recalls a free-spirited atmosphere in the studio when it came time to record the album, something which was the modus operandi for all the recording sessions to which he contributed. "There was no structure to it and it was completely left up to the bass players to come up with something, a typical day in the studio was always: start at 10 o'clock and Benny would sit at the piano and play the song to us, and what the chords were, then we'd go on from there and we'd work to lunch. About one o'clock we would resume. There were never any night sessions with Björn and Benny. We'd finish at six or seven o'clock in the evening, and if we didn't have that song ready, then we'd continue the next day. Sometimes it'd take two days just to do the bass and drums. Everything else was put on later, but in the studio, it would be the guitar, bass, drums, and Björn would sit on a chair with the acoustic singing the song and we'd go from there just making everything up."

As a ten-year-old there was not one weak track on that album. In other words, it was all killer, no filler. The crowning glory and the centrepiece of the album was, and still remains to this day for me, 'SOS'. It is arguably the greatest pop song ever written. Both The Who's Pete Townsend and John Lennon praised the song. The song even inspired the Sex Pistols, as bassist Glen Matlock revealed in his book, *I Was a Teenage Sex Pistol*, where 'SOS' provided the bare bones to the Pistols' 'Pretty Vacant' after he heard the song playing on a jukebox. 'SOS' is a master class in song-writing, production and arrangement; the interplay between musical dynamics: light and dark, happiness and sadness. Interestingly, Matlock's successor on bass in Sex Pistols, Sid Vicious, was also a huge fan of ABBA. There is even a story of the occasion where Vicious encountered Agnetha and Frida at Stockholm airport and expressed his admiration of the band to them.

Watson is also one of several non-Swedish born musicians

to have contributed to ABBA recordings. The Englishman's musical journey to ABBA began in the sixties when the band he was in at the time set out to Sweden for a tour. "In 1964 the band I was in, The Hi-Grades, got an offer to come to Sweden to back American singer Larry Finnegan," he explains. "We then came back the next year with Swedish rock 'n' roll star, Jerry Williams. But when the band split up I stayed in Sweden and began working with different pop bands. I then met Björn and Benny while on a tour, they were playing at different venues to us and we partied after a show. I later started playing with Björn and Benny before they became ABBA, because they became producers for Polar Records and they started using Rutger and I for those productions which ultimately led to working on the ABBA recordings.

"In those days we were like 'The Wrecking Crew'* of Sweden. We were like three bass players, three drummers and a few guitar players and pianists. And we had all the session work that was going on because we were in the studio maybe three or four days a week in the seventies and eighties."

Abba would reach superstar status in 1976 when the group would spend almost two thirds of the year at the top of the Australian charts with three singles; 'Fernando', 'Dancing Queen' and 'Money, Money, Money'. Following ABBA's breakthrough, other Swedish bands took the Aussie charts by storm: Harpo appeared on our airwaves with 'Moviestar' in 1976, which peaked at #3 on the Australian charts and featured ABBA's Frida on backing vocals, and then a few years later Ted Gärdestad had a minor hit with 'Take Me Back to Hollywood', as well as new wave popsters Secret Service and their single 'Oh Susie' which peaked at #49 on the Australian chart.

"When it came to success in Australia, we found out after a while and were very happy that the song was liked on the other side of the globe," remembers Ulf Wahlberg, keyboardist,

---

* A famed American group of session musicians who appeared on countless popular music recordings during the 1960s

vocalist and producer with Secret Service. "We were hoping to do a tour there, but unfortunately it never happened. The reason being, because there was a lot of touring and TV appearances all over Europe and South America, there was really no time. In addition, [Secret Service vocalist] Ola Håkansson and I were also very busy with our other careers, me as record producer and songwriter and Ola as publishing manager at the record company Sonet Records."

In the wake of ABBA's worldwide success, an explosion of Swedish pop and rock acts then took hold on the international stage with acts such as Europe, Roxette, Ace of Base, Avicii and Swedish House Mafia achieving commercial success. "ABBA's success meant a lot for Swedish music exports" affirms Wahlberg, "before ABBA, Swedish popular music was in principle only widespread in Scandinavia and to some extent Germany. With ABBA, the interest in Swedish-produced music became enormous all over the world. Sweden has always had a good quality of creators in pop/rock music. Now they finally got the chance to be heard and seen."

"I believe that ABBA's worldwide success played a huge role in putting Sweden on the map" concurs Ian Haugland, drummer with Swedish rockers Europe. "They were the first band out of the country to gain global recognition, and they were also the first band to have a working global network, with record companies, managements and concert promoters. They definitely opened the doors to the world for all music out of Sweden, no matter what genre!"

Mike Watson agrees: "ABBA opened up doors for Swedish music, and for the likes of Max Martin and all the producers and songwriters that's come out of Sweden since. And considering that, back in the day, all the newspapers in Sweden thought ABBA were like a bubble gum band, where they would be here today, and gone tomorrow."

****

In the early part of 1990s Swedish dance-pop group Ace of Base were one of the biggest selling acts in Australia. Both their singles, 1992's 'All That She Wants' and 1993's 'The Sign' topped the Australian charts, with 'All That She Wants' selling 120,000 copies alone and 'The Sign' 95,000 copies. The commercial success of the group boosted the fortunes of Australian record label Possum Records.

"I heard the band's first single 'All That She Wants' when I was attending MIDEM in Nice, France," recalls Philip Israel, owner of Possum, who signed the band in 1992. "At that time they'd only had success in Scandinavia. They attended MIDEM to try and get their debut album *Happy Nation* released in other countries. I heard it and thought it could be a hit, so I signed the band. It was the most important signing to Possum Records and helped establish us as a serious independent Australian record company."

The popularity of Ace Of Base saw them go onto become the third-largest selling Swedish music act behind Roxette and ABBA. "Both ABBA and Roxette are still going strong record sales-wise whereas Ace of Base will go down in music history as a two-hit wonder," confirms Israel. "The biggest mistake they made was to believe the hype from a major record company and they left the independent record company and signed with Universal worldwide. They probably did get a bit of money from Universal, but all of a sudden they were just another band in an enormous artist roster and that was the end of Ace of Base."

My enchantment with Sweden was given a further boost in 1995 when I played lead guitar in an award-winning local theatre stage production of *Chess*, the musical written by ABBA's Björn Ulvaeus and Benny Andersson and lyricist Tim Rice. So, the Swedish connection continued to synchronize for me. My next connection with the country came in 2001 when, having moved to Melbourne to pursue my music career on a full-time basis, a copy of Swedish punk rockers Backyard Babies' new album arrived on my desk courtesy of BMG. *Making Enemies Is*

Good had gone straight to number one in their native Sweden and had opened the doors to international success. This led to the band heading down under for their first ever tour of Australia in July. It had taken them twelve years to achieve their first number one album, and the new album would also earn them another Grammy award (their first was for their 1998 album *Total 13*). They had opened for AC/DC in the latter part of 2000 on the European leg of their worldwide tour in support of *Stiff Upper Lip*. So the band's trajectory was certainly on the up. Like their previous album, the new album was also produced by someone who would later become a mainstay of my musical circle, Tomas Skogsberg.

I spoke to the band's lead vocalist and guitarist Nicke Borg the day after their arrival in Melbourne. With a heavy schedule, the interview was conducted via phone. He mentioned that they were settling in well, having enjoyed a night of fine food and drink at inner seaside suburban St Kilda. I was among the audience when the band played a show at the Corner Hotel in Richmond and witnessed a truly great rock and roll performance. The heavily-tattooed lead guitar, Dregen, and Borg certainly epitomized the spirit of rock and roll, a subject matter that I had asked Borg about in our interview.

"I think you can't do what we do if you don't really believe in it or what you are, I'm not sleeping with leather pants on and doing a line of cocaine the first thing in the morning and then drink Jack Daniels for breakfast. But if you do that, I think you'll die anyway really! I never found anything glorious in a rock and roll death, but I don't like people singing about shit like that and who don't know what they're talking about. There's lots of bands around that are thinking they can sell records by singing about cocaine and they've only smoked a joint when they were 16! So, you must be really solid and honest because I think a kid today can actually look through that and we try to be very nonpolitical and take no responsibility for anything. We're just a rock band the way it should be, a bit scary, a bit dangerous and outrageous."

How I eventually came to tour Sweden and develop friendships and professional relationships was largely due to the helpful persistence of two Swedish fans of mine who had first become fans of my music upon release of my first studio outing, *Slave to The Fingers* in 2011 and my first European tour in 2012. They were largely responsible for bringing me to the attention of a local Swedish musician and local promoter who had recently toured with Sweet and Slade in Sweden, but it would take several years before the Swedish tour would come to fruition, with said promoter finally signing me up to bring me to Sweden for my first tour there in October 2017. That inaugural tour opened many opportunities, from eventually joining the promoter's own Stockholm-based hard rock band Rough Rockers as guitarist to being introduced to acclaimed Swedish producer and the godfather of Swedish death metal Tomas Skogsberg with whom I've since gone on to work. As a member of Rough Rockers, we signed to Dutch indie RVP Records, who released our EP, *Smoke and Mirrors* in early 2019.

The story of how Janne Schaffer, legendary Swedish guitarist who, alongside fellow Swedish guitarist Lasse Wellander, were the two mainstay session guitarists on many of ABBA's iconic recordings and me, an Australian guitarist, came to work with each other, is an interesting tale. It all started when I was on my second tour of Sweden in May 2019. During my stay in Stockholm I had visited a local record store, The Beat Goes On, located on Sankt Eriksgatan and a few doors down from the original site of Polar Studios, ABBA's recording studio which itself had been housed in an old cinema building. The record store owner Lars had booked me for an in-store acoustic performance. Whilst I was perusing his array of vinyls and CDs, I noticed some early Janne Schaffer albums on his shelves, and Lars began telling me about how Janne was a regular visitor to his store. We began chatting about all things ABBA and about Janne's illustrious playing career. Lars told me that Janne and I had lots in common when it came to a love of instrumental guitar music. Early on in my career I had recorded and released several instrumental guitar albums in the early 2010s, so these albums shared much in common with Janne's, and while mine were more in the rock vein, Janne's were more heavily jazz-prog-rock infused outings and albums that garnered him much widespread acclaim both in Sweden and worldwide.

In 1973 Janne's eponymous debut album had gone to number one on the Swedish music charts, outselling ABBA that particular year, who had just released their debut album, *Ring, Ring* and which only managed to reach number two on the same chart! Janne was, and remains, a highly-respected session guitarist who has played guitar on albums by such music legends as Johnny Nash and Bob Marley. He is also the recipient of a Swedish Grammy, known locally as The Grammis, which he received in 1989 for his album *Electric Graffiti*, which was issued on his own label, Earmeal. He had earned the award for 'Instrumental Production of the Year'.

On the day of my in-store I arrived to prepare for my performance, and a small group of people were already taking their positions in the store. Lars informed me that Janne had visited his store earlier that day to purchase some recordings and Lars took it upon himself to mention that an Australian guitarist was in town and performing and that he too had recorded instrumental guitar albums. He played Janne some of my material and Janne liked what he heard and, though he expressed an interest in wanting to meet me, he told Lars that he had a gig later that evening and was unable to come to the instore and catch my show but asked him to personally pass on his best regards and to let me know much he enjoyed my guitar work. Lars later informed me of Janne's message, which came as a surprise and was such a compliment coming from such an esteemed guitar legend as Janne Schaffer. It certainly made my day.

Back in Australia, I later connected with Janne and thanked him for the message he had left for me. I told him how much respect and admiration I had for his guitar work both with ABBA and his own solo outings. At the same time, I was working on a new song, 'Take A Look' which I was in the middle of recording, and during one of our conversations, I mentioned to Janne whether he was interested in guesting on guitar on the track. When he said he would love to play guitar with me on the track, a rush of excitement ran through my body.

Janne ended up playing lead guitar throughout the song, while I played rhythm guitar. Entering a local studio, Crunch Studio in Stockholm, Janne, armed with his signature Canadian made Larrivée guitar, improvised a breathtaking guitar solo which took the track to the next level. His soulful, smooth and creamy guitar tone proved the perfect match for the song. Janne has a sixth sense, he knows exactly what a song needs, and he delivered that in spades on my track. "Playing on your song and whenever I play on other artist's music, always inspires me to try out new ideas and see what other people like," he told me. Having Janne play on my track solidified my Swedish connection even further. The other musicians on the track, Janne Borgh on bass and Manne Åström on drums, were also Swedish along with producer Tomas Skogsberg. During that tour in 2019 I would spend two days at Tomas' Sunlight Studios recording a couple of tracks which I documented in my previous book, *Backstage Pass: The Grit and the Glamour*.

Born on September 24, 1945, in Blackeberg, a suburb in the western section of Stockholm, both Janne's parents were musicians, their passion for music imbued him with a life love of music which eventually led to an interest in the guitar. His first guitar was an acoustic he built himself while still in high school. He eventually picked up an electric guitar and hearing John Mayall and The Bluesbreakers with Eric Clapton in 1966 proved a pivotal point in his playing trajectory. He soon played guitar in a succession of local bands before joining Sleepstones. "We did some small recordings, but nothing much else," he recalls, "we copied the English bands, mostly Yardbirds, and Eric Clapton." The band would provide the young up-and-coming guitarist with a platform to refine his musicianship as well as provide him with valuable experience in opening for international bands touring Sweden.

One of the bands Sleepstones ended up supporting was Cliff Richard and The Shadows. "It was at a theatre called Chinateatern [The China Theatre] in Stockholm, they were very polite, and it was very clean music. I liked Hank Marvin's guitar sound; you could immediately hear him play and recognize him, but he just played melodies. But he didn't improvise so much which was what I was into more. My style of playing was more along the lines of Clapton, Jeff Beck and Jimi Hendrix."

On another occasion Sleepstones shared the stage with Jimi Hendrix and The Byrds. "It was part of a theatre programme in Stockholm that featured Sleepstones, Jimi Hendrix and The Byrds on the same bill," he says. "Jimi was fantastic but at the time he wasn't in his best shape because he had been taking some drugs so wasn't starting the concert in his best form. After about half an hour, the promoter wanted to end his concert, but Jimi said 'no, I'm not finished yet'. He started getting angry, but it was only then that he really started to play, and he played for two hours. And it was just fantastic and a memorable concert."

With the late 1960s a hive of both cultural and musical activity, in between playing music, Janne would catch the latest touring act passing through Stockholm. "I saw The Rolling Stones, The Doors, The Band and so many others. The Mothers of Invention with Frank Zappa was a memorable concert for me too as Zappa told the Swedish audience, 'Since you don't understand my lyrics at all, I will just perform the whole concert as an instrumental' and that's what he did and it was just fantastic."

Eventually Janne tired of Sleepstones and moved onto his next band, Grapes of Wrath, which featured future ABBA session drummer Ola Brunkert, before leaving that too to form Opus III. A chance to support Björn Skifs brought an offer to play guitar on a recording session which would become the springboard for him becoming an in-demand studio session player.

"The first real recording session I did was with Björn Skifs on his 1970 album *From Both Sides,* and after that session everybody started calling me for lots of session work and recording with a lot of Swedish artists. And, at the same time, Benny Andersson and Björn Ulvaeus were hired as producers by Polar Records and hired me to play guitar on Ted Gärdestad's first album, *Undringar,* which we recorded in 1971. This was the first real record I played on. Before the album saw release in 1972, Benny and Björn asked me to play on 'People Need Love' which became the debut ABBA recording, though the single was released under the name of 'Björn & Benny, Agnetha & Anni-Frid'. [The debut single was released in June 1972]. From then on, my guitar playing appeared on every ABBA album except for 1981's *The Visitors* in 1981 and 2021's *Voyage.*"

With his session work keeping him extremely busy, he had to decline the offer to go on tour with ABBA, instead recommending another guitar-playing friend, Lasse Wellander, who accepted the offer and would go on to hit the stages with the band on all their tours between 1975 to 1980 and contribute guitar on all their albums too.

Alongside his burgeoning session career, Janne also embarked on a solo career, with his eponymous debut album finally seeing the light of day in Sweden in 1973. His reputation would soon garner international attention, with interest from overseas labels. In England his first album was retitled and issued under the name of *The Chinese* albeit with a different track listing. "With my first album that I had recorded and released in Sweden, it had a blues tune called, 'Did You Ever Love a Woman' that Slim Notini sang on," explains Janne, "but the label in England didn't like it, so they asked me, 'could you add an instrumental?' I had already recorded a tune called 'The Chinese' — which Björn J:son Lindh played keyboards on — and so we added that track and another one I had, and retitled my first album in England, *The Chinese* after that tune."

Janne's fifty-year career saw him adhere to a busy schedule of recording sessions for various artists, plus his own solo outings. Having a deep and strong passion for guitar playing he has never found any interest in chasing the fickleness of fame or fortune. For Janne, it's always been about the love for the instrument and the desire to perform to an audience that keeps his creative flame burning brightly.

"I'm interested in the music only," he says, "I've never been interested in drugs. I have a couple of friends who did the drugs and they're no longer alive. I don't think I would improve my playing by taking drugs, it would only take me in another direction and the playing would get worse and worse. I have a passion for playing music and will try to do it as long as I can. As long as I can stand up and play the songs without any problems, I will continue to do so, but if I notice that I have some problems to remember things and so on, then maybe I will do something else."

As Sweden's number one session guitarist, Janne's guitar work has appeared on over 5,000 recordings since his first studio session in 1970. Yet one session stands out as his most memorable. "It was for an instrumental written by my best friend Björn J:son Lindh called 'Brusa Högre Lilla Å' or loosely translated in English it is called 'Sing Louder Little River', he reveals. "In the studio Björn gave me a piece of paper with a lot of notes on it and I asked him how do you want me to play? And he said, 'you can figure that out yourself' and so I did that, and I did two live takes on that tune and the second was the take we kept. And it became one of the biggest hits in Sweden and a track I still play at every concert I perform, with the track having become very popular and often played at weddings and funerals."

1977 would prove to be a busy year for Schaffer with the release of *Katharsis*, the first of three acclaimed jazz-fusion albums that he would record for Columbia Records in America (the albums would appear on CBS Records in the UK and Europe). In the wake of the release of *Katharsis*, Columbia sent over two of its A&R people to Stockholm to catch a live performance by Schaffer, and later invited him to America to record his next album, *Earmeal* (1979), in Los Angeles. That record also featured the Porcaro family; Jeff on drums, Steve on keyboard, Mike on bass and their father Joe on percussion, one of the rare occasions where all the Porcaro family played together on an album outside of Toto. The album was also produced by Bruce Botnik, who is most famously associated with The Doors. One of the tracks on the album, 'It's Never Too Late', would later be sampled by American rapper KRS-One in 1992 for his track 'Like a Throttle'.

In 1980 the last of the trilogy of CBS albums was released. *Presens* was only issued in Europe. Also, that same year, he formed the Electric Banana Band, a catchy funk-house-rock orientated combo aimed at entertaining children with the band members all wearing jungle themed costumes. The Electric Banana Band, who sometimes shortened the name to EBB — echoes of Electric Light Orchestra's acronym of ELO — write songs aimed at children with an important environmental message that are very accessible to young audiences within a playful atmospheric stage show. The group have a cult following that span several generations, and over the past forty years the group has released a swathe of best-selling albums, and entertained generations of Swedish children. Fronted by well-known Swedish actor, film director and artist Lasse Åberg, the first band came together from the enormous popularity of a late 1970s Swedish children television program titled *Trazan & Banarne* which starred Åberg in the lead role.

In 2018 American pop star Christina Aguilera sampled Janne's track 'No Registration' which appeared on his debut album, for her song, 'Sick of Sittin'' which appears on her *Liberation* album.

2023 saw the fiftieth anniversary of Janne's debut topping the Swedish charts, and it holds an ever more special relevance for him. "Fifty years ago, I topped the Swedish chart for six weeks and during the last week I was at number one, Sweden got a new king," he says. "So, in 2023 the Swedish king celebrated 50 years on the throne, and I celebrated fifty years of topping the chart in the same year for my first album. And that's a coincidence but what a special coincidence it is."

Janne Schaffer is considered a musical legend in his native Sweden. Every Swedish musician knows his name and his body of work. His status as a national treasure is such that he has even performed at the inauguration of the Swedish Parliament as well as before the royal family and Prime Minister. I remember the excitement expressed by producer Tomas Skogsberg when we were working on 'Take A Look' that Janne was contributing guitar. Tomas had told me that he had grown up listening to Janne's work and so admired and respected him — he was such an inspiring musical hero. He felt, just as I did, that it was such a huge honour to be working with him.

Janne has a giving soul and is passionate about helping young musicians and up and coming musicians and believes nurturing the next generation is vital to building a strong and healthy creative music community. A pure, gentle, selfless and humble soul whose love of music is infectious. In his native Sweden he worked hard and passionately to set up foundations in memory of Björn J:son Lindh and Ted Gärdestad allowing a platform for grants to be given to new, young and talented musicians. Janne, together with famed Swedish jazz guitarist Rune Gustafsson, played a major role in campaigning to make electric guitar playing a viable option in the national curriculum of music schools throughout Sweden.

In his fifty-plus year career as a guitar player, Janne has always strived to evolve musically and is never one to repeat himself. He's always looking forward. "If you go back and listen to my first solo album and then listen to my most current music I've released, you will hear a big difference in the way my playing and music has developed and in the way I also write music. I never wanted to get stuck in a special formula, I want to always experiment and do new things."

In June 2023, Janne was bestowed the 'Litteris et Artibus' medal for outstanding artistic contributions within Swedish music by His Majesty the King at Stockholm Royal Palace.

Translated from the Latin that means Science and Art in English and is a medal first instituted in 1853 by Crown Prince Carl for outstanding artistic contributions mainly within music, dramatic art, and literature.

That same year Schaffer would finally reunite with Agnetha Fältskog when the latter tapped him to contribute guitar to 'Past Forever' a song on Fältskog's tenth anniversary reissue of her 2013 album *A*. The new 2023 version, titled *A+*, featured the original ten tracks reworked and re-imagined with the addition of a new track, 'Where Do We Go From Here?'

"I am really proud to record again with Agnetha," Schaffer said, "I did the recording of my guitar in October 2022 at the album's producer Jörgen Elofsson's home on Lidingö. And though Agnetha was not present, I did meet her later at one of my concerts I performed in the summer of 2023 where we talked about it and she told me that she was very satisfied."

And, continuing our connection, in 2023 Janne and I co-wrote and recorded an instrumental titled 'Continental Meeting' that writer and music journalist Mick Middles described as, "a blistering, ferocious tune that returns to the distant and fine art of the 'guitar instrumental' that evokes echoes the '70s instrumental fury of Focus spliced with shards of Jeff Beck and Ten Years After".

****

On my 2017 tour of Sweden, I finally got a chance to visit the original site of ABBA's Polar Studios on Sankt Eriksgatan, the place where Janne spent much time on those ABBA recording sessions. The studio was only 400 metres from where I had played a show a couple of evenings prior, at a venue called Klubb BLA. Before Polar Studios began operating as a recording studio in 1978, the building had been a former cinema built sometime around 1930. The site sits next to the Sankt Eriksbron bridge, and at the time of my visit, the building housed a gymnasium on the first floor as the studio had closed in 2004.

My Swedish connection has brought me many cherished

memories. One such memory was another show I performed on that same 2017 tour, this time at a venue called Bomber Bar in the heart of Motala which sits about a three-hour drive southwest of Stockholm and is positioned on the eastern side of Lake Vättern, the second largest lake in Sweden. Primarily a metal venue, the bar is located a few steps from the Vättern lakeside which provided me with a postcard view. I was supporting a metal act, and initially was hesitant in doing the show, as the type of acoustic music I was performing in solo mode was not a perfect fit for that type of audience. Yet to my surprise my set was well received, and I was later informed that it provided a nice change to their usual fare and was the perfect warm up act to gently ease in the enthused Swedish metal crowd.

At that show one of the funniest moments in my touring life occurred. It was while I and several members of the metal band were seated and enjoying our dinner in the front bar area, when suddenly a van pulled up outside the venue, and parked itself in front of the front bar window where we sat. The first thought that came to mind was that it was a band who may have been double booked since they were not familiar to us or any other people in the venue. Instead three young musicians, each with their instruments in hand set up inside the van with portable amps, including a drum set, and with the van's sliding door wide open, broke out into spontaneous song and began playing away. They even had homemade pyro on the roof going off, it was a hilarious and spectacular performance with many of the venue punters taking out their phones and filming it all. We all broke out into laughter. It was one of the most unique ways for a band to get noticed. I'm sure if an A & R person happened to be there that night, that band would certainly have captured their undivided attention.

And, as fate would have it, I ended signing to Possum Records in late 2022, and the label released my all-instrumental album, *The Lone Runner* in early 2023. The album went on to debut on the Australian ARIA Jazz and Blues chart at No.4, awarding me my first ever Top 10 album. The album would stay in the Top 10 for three consecutive weeks.

8: Everybody's Got To Learn Sometime

My entire decade of schooling was soundtracked by the music of the 1970s, and then as I entered the workforce at the start of 1981, having dropped out of school at fifteen, the music of the eighties would leave a mark on me as well. Those two decades in music proved to be an influential period upon me, shaping the direction of my life forever. I wasn't old enough to have experienced the enormous cultural changes that arose from the creative spirit of the 1960s which affected everything from music to fashion to advances in technology. The aftermath of The Beatles arrival upon the scene was an epoch-defining moment that changed the musical landscape permanently. Everything that followed in their wake would owe a large debt to the band. From various studio recording techniques to musical compositions and, at its basic form, the influence upon the formation of multitude of bands.

As music and fashion tends to run in cycles, the early eighties saw a second wave of British music dominate and influence the sounds of what would follow. Just as The Beatles, The Rolling Stones, The Kinks, The Animals and others formed the first British Invasion in the early 1960s, affecting massive changes upon the musical landscape, so did the synthesized and electronic sounds of the Second British Invasion bands such as Duran Duran, Eurythmics, The Human League and many others opened the flood gates, giving the sonic paintbrush to artists to add electronic elements to their music. Even the bands that previously relied heavily on the standard guitar, bass and drum template, started adding flourishes of synthesized elements to their musical creations. As the electronic sounds engrained themselves into the cultural landscape, even heavy metal bands would begin experimenting with synthesizers, with

MTV providing the visual platform for this new movement.

Bands that previously had been the hit-makers of the day, who were now considered by to be dinosaurs, began to reappear and achieve a second wind of success thanks to electronic music, while others were never able to replicate their initial success. Time had moved on and tastes had changed. One band that experienced a rebirth was English prog-rock outfit The Moody Blues. Having last topped the charts in 1972, the group returned with all guns blazing in 1981 with their tenth studio outing *Long Distance Voyager.*

"If I could just choose one decade of music, it would be the 80s," Moody Blues' singer, songwriter and guitarist Justin Hayward told me in an interview. "For us we had *Long Distance Voyager* and that was great. But after that, we really needed to find a producer that was solid, and I met Tony Visconti at the BBC as we were both asked to do a project there and I thought Tony would be the ideal person for The Moodies. And so, I asked him and we recorded two or three albums at his studio: *The Other Side of Life* (1986) which was where 'Wildest Dreams' came from, and *Sur la Mer* (1988) which was where 'I Know You're Out There Somewhere' came from.

"A very disciplined producer would work from 11 till 7 and that was it, even if you were in the middle of a take he'd walk out, but not Tony. So I loved the way Tony worked. He was a bass player too, and he was the first producer I knew to sync things up, like through MIDI stuff. For us that mid 80s period with 'Wildest Dreams' was the most wonderful time. The first-time round with the success in the 60s and 70s, I'd missed it because my mind was elsewhere; chemically, mystically, and emotionally, but in the 80s I was straight, aware, alive, and awake to all of this wonderful stuff. It was such a joy and such a gift to have that opportunity again especially when you are 40 years old, it was such a blessing."

****

I found the latter part of the seventies in particular a glorious period for music. Music provided me with a form of expression and an outlet and escape from the everyday life. And the wealth of music on offer and the diversity of styles that were played on radio allowed for many bands and artists to be discovered by music fans. Unlike today, where formatted radio stations have one main central office curating the programming and non-varied music that is played infinitum whilst sticking to what is considered the latest trend in music, the DJs back then were passionate music lovers who, if a song was to their liking, they would freely air it.

A case in point is Queen's 'Bohemian Rhapsody' which, thanks to radio DJ Kenny Everett's enthusiasm, stormed the charts after he played an advance copy of the song 14 times over the course of two days on his Capital Radio show, forever changing the fortunes of the band. Now stations with a classic rock format are the closest you'll get to that type of radio programming. Record companies with big budgets can spoon feed station MDs with their priority acts in order to keeping the dollar-making machine well-oiled, while lesser bands, or those without a big label behind them, never get a look in.

I was in my second last year of high school when the sublime sounds of an infectious tune on the radio caught my ears. One cold winter's morning as I was preparing to head out to school a flurry of piano notes, that to my ears sounded like a piece of classical music having time-travelled far into the future, a future I was now part of, opened the tune, before a choir of drums, bass and guitar joined in as the vocalist began singing, "Hey mama it's a long, long way…". I waited with bated breath for the radio announcer to reveal the name once the song had ended. "That was the new single 'Halfway Hotel' by English group Voyager" chimed the radio DJ. This was the first I had ever heard of the band.

The following Sunday evening, as was part of the ritual of every Australian teenager back then, television music program *Countdown*, our country's answer to Britain's *Top of The Pops*, aired the video of the song. I sat transfixed by the cryptic imagery. The band set up and performing in a hotel while some strange, mask-wearing clientele roamed its stairways and hallways. A young couple entered the hotel's premises and were greeted by an assortment of characters who mysteriously stared at the couple, then flicked laser beams between each other's eyes. Part sci-fi, part otherworldly, it made for a strange juxtaposition between the song's subject matter and the video's imagery.

Oh, the power of video. Once seen, one can never undo that initial vision. It's forever etched in one's memory. Regardless, it was an earworm of a song. Even today as I write this, the song's melody begins playing in my head and continues to play. 'Halfway Hotel' is well-crafted, well-performed and meticulously arranged. The song's chordal sequence is very clever. Genius in fact. More sophisticated chords such as Major sevenths, diminished seventh chords and ninths are married to the standard major and minor chordal fare. And though the song would prove to be the band's only major hit, thus forever labelling them a one hit wonder, look into the band's history and you'll find there's a lot more undiscovered gold to be found. And although Voyager's time in the limelight was brief, their influence went well beyond a hit record for this then fourteen-year-old, it proved another pivotal moment in my music journey.

Before coming into existence as Voyager, vocalist/keyboardist Paul French had already spent a decade recording and touring in a number of groups, first as a member in pop outfit Windmill, and later as a member of prog-jazz-rock band Tonton Macoute which saw them signed to Neon Records, an imprint of RCA, recording and releasing their only self-titled album in June 1971. The album has gone on to become a much sought after collector's item due to the fact Neon Records only ever released eleven copies of the album in the UK in their label's short one year existence.

In early 1977 French got together with bassist Chris Hook and drummer Humberto "Bertie" Bradley to form The Paul

French Connection. In the summer of 1977 the group entered the studio, together with producer Tony Hatch and a session guitarist, to record an early version of 'Halfway Hotel' a song French had written, along with a B-side, 'When I Need a Friend' which would also re-appear on the group's third self-titled album. The Paul French Connection's version of 'Halfway Hotel' was later released on Arista Records but failed to attract any attention.

In the aftermath of the single's failure, The Paul French Connection morphed into Voyager in 1978 — the name taken from the space craft that launched in 1977 — with Paul Hirsh having joined the group on guitar and keyboards. "Being introduced to the music of the Paul French Connection was a world away from the rock/pop bands in Newbury, Berkshire I'd played with when living there in 1977/8," recalls Hirsh on his joining. "There was blues and a soulful element elevated by jazz harmonies in this pot-pourri of prog and an English orchestral quality in some compositions, that reminded me of composer Edward Elgar. I'd just moved back to London, so travelled to Newbury once a week for an evening rehearsal, stay overnight then back the next morning. It was an exciting and musically inspiring time, and I learned a lot while getting to know the guys and contributing to the arrangements, particularly when a new song from the prolific Mr French arrived even though the future was uncertain."

The group built up a solid following in their native Berkshire, and were eventually spotted by the management of Scottish band Nazareth who signed the band to their Mountain Records label.

"Most bands would not get a look in with record companies unless they were gigging regularly and building a fanbase," recalls Paul French today, "we were certainly playing live a lot around Newbury where we all lived and had quite a local following, so A&R men coming to see us would see that we were going down well. After a couple of visits by Derek Nicol, MD of Mountain Records, we were signed up to the label early in 1978. Our manager was a guy named Paul Walden and they were both keen for us to keep gigging once the album was recorded with Gus Dudgeon producing."

By this point they had refined their earlier prog-rock template to a more pop friendly format and would also record a new version of 'Halfway Hotel' for their debut album of the same name which they began recording over a two-month period in late 1978. "The album was recorded with Gus Dudgeon producing at his studio The Mill at Cookham in Berkshire," recalls French. "Gus was known for his meticulous production and every performance was fully scrutinised. I felt that a lot of the spontaneity and feel were lost sometimes because of that. But he was the man very much in charge, so everything was done his way.

"Bertie was with us when we first went into the studio with Gus, but, as Gus wanted a heavier approach to the drums, Bertie decided to leave. As a result, it was a session drummer who tried to overdub the drums on the newly-recorded Voyager version of 'Halfway Hotel' without success. At this point, Johnny Marter joined us and solved the drummer problems."

"When we first went into The Mill to do our first tracks with Gus, we did 'Halfway Hotel', a B side and another track," concurs Paul Hirsh. "Then Gus decided that we needed to change drummer, but we'd already recorded 'Halfway Hotel'. So we wiped the original drums off and John Marter came in and dubbed the drums over it without any click or metronome. He just did it and got it perfect. We had also just purchased the first Yamaha CP70 Piano — on credit — giving the group a realistic sound and portability. Gus suggested buying this new synth, The Yamaha CS80 which was big, heavy and expensive, to inspire new songs and sounds. I believe we were the first to get it imported from Japan and the polyphonic touch sensitivity and big fat brassy stingy textures became a standard from then on."

"We stayed over during weekdays," adds French. "The place was quite luxurious. But I was an early riser and still am.

Gus on the other hand didn't start work 'til at least 3pm and would then work through to 3 or 4 am. I found that difficult, as I would be ready to start work at 10am, so I had minimal sleep and would be hanging around for long periods. Don't get me wrong though, because Gus was a great character and could be very entertaining and good fun to work with. The band had a good rapport musically, so rehearsals were always fun and exciting. We all knew when something was right, and disagreements were rare."

In advance of the album's release, the title track was issued as the lead single, and would climb all the way to #15 on the Australian chart, while in England it peaked just inside the Top 40 at #33.

"We rapidly went to No.1 in the airplay chart but owing to problems with the pressing plant, who prioritised EMI, we went to the back of the queue so that fans could not buy it immediately," recalls French. "That's the reason we did not climb very high over in the UK! We did get a few prestige gigs arranged by the record company to play before music press, such as The Venue in London's Victoria. Then later we played various festivals in Europe booked on the strength of the single and album material. Van Morrison headlined one we played in Belgium and Queen headlined a big festival in Saarbrucken. Nowadays I believe acts make decent money from live appearances, but back then the record company had to pay to get us on tours and ultimately took the costs from any royalties we might receive. And during this period, we were put on a modest weekly wage and of course we were expected to give interviews and be at management/record company's beck and call generally."

Encouraged by the success of 'Halfway Hotel', the group turned their focus on trying to break into the lucrative American market. "Unfortunately, our album came out the same week that Elektra Records brought out albums by Joni Mitchell and The Eagles at the same time, so we didn't get a look in," reveals Hirsh. "Not only that, but we never went over to the US to promote. Our forte was songs and studio. Paul French was really a songwriter, a man with a love of jazz and classical music, who was also a conductor, arranger and composer, but loved the pop stuff too. He could do it all. His craft was creating songs and recording with vocals his specialty. Piano, bass and drums was the basis for nearly all these songs. Playing live was another thing altogether, particularly with a band with that kind of material. It's not easy to just go out there and just lay it down in front of a crowd. It needs a little bit of thought, which is why I suggested having two more people, but we weren't really a strong live band. We didn't put our focus into playing live. We did it and enjoyed it, but it never really had a groove."

As for the 'Halfway Hotel' video, "I have no idea what that was about," admits French. "I wanted something to do with the story in the song, but Storm Thorgerson of Hipgnosis fame, thought not. He was given free reign by management and record company and what you have seen was the result. It was filmed in the Grosvenor Hotel (now known as the Clermont) by Victoria station in London. Personally, I think it was uninspired and also it was expensive to make. I'm pretty sure Storm got involved because it paid the rent. The video we did for 'Judas' was a lot better I think and was a lot cheaper too."

"I didn't particularly like it either," adds Hook, "it was weird, but it was Storm Thorgerson who came up with the ideas. And I think because he had such a big name, management wanted him to do it because it would be great, but videos were in their infancy at that time."

"It was this new film technology that these guys were experimenting with, superimposing little graphic images over live footage," adds Hirsh. "And the idea was it was all about eye contact. It was about people giving certain looks to other people, so these little lines going across the screen were the line of one person's eye looking into another across the room and giving them, whatever look they were giving them. They got all these actors in with funny faces and dressed up in fancy stuff. It was very primitive digital technology at that time."

In the press the band were often compared to Queen and Genesis due to some of the songs on the album being almost mini operas in composition such as the dystopian epic 'Captain Remus' while with others such as 'Halfway Hotel', were a more straightforward pop direction was taken, a perfect match for radio.

The group then embarked on their first tour in support of their debut album in 1979, which took in a club and university tour of the UK, then two shows in mainland Europe; an open air rock festival on August 18 at Saarbrucken Germany, where Queen headlined, and other acts included Molly Hatchet, Rory Gallagher, Alvin Lee (10 Years After) and The Commodores, followed by the next day, August 19, at the Bilzen festival in Belgium which was headlined by Van Morrison, and included Nils Lofgren among others.

The same year also saw Voyager perform a BBC Radio One Concert as support to heavy rock group Gillan and an appearance on UK's *Top of The Pops* television program as well as a performance on German popular music TV show. The group would again perform a BBC Radio One Concert the following year, this time as support for Chris Rea.

Things were also looking bright for the band in America, until an unfortunate turn of events changed their fortunes. "I don't think we had brilliant management, to be honest," muses Hook, "he was an inexperienced manager and was only a year or so older than us and, though very ambitious, he could have organised things a lot better that way. Mountain Records and our management and Derek Nicol, who ran the label, were very keen on the band, but their focus was on Britain and America. We had a deal with Elektra/Asylum in America and the CEO of Elektra/Asylum at the time was Bob Krasnow. He was very keen on the band, and so things were looking very exciting for us in America. But then Bob had some kind of breakdown and disappeared off into the mountains to his cabin and later got fired. Unfortunately, any project of Bob's was bad news at Elecktra/Asylum. So the album just got sent out in a brown paper cover to the radio stations. It could have been big in America, but it the timing was wrong. We were just unlucky in that sense."

Upon completion of the tours Voyager returned to the studio in late 1979 to begin work on the follow-up album which would be titled *Act of Love* and would see release in 1980. Having already shored up an abundance of songs for the second album, and with the group evolving musically, the group focused on recording a more elaborate outing whilst still purposely keeping to a more pop oriented template to build upon the momentum created by the success of *Halfway Hotel*.

While the band were busy recording, a second single, 'Judas', was issued from their debut album which peaked at #93 on the Australian charts. "We were in the middle of recording the second album when we filmed the 'Judas' video," recalls Hook. "We were sort of dragged out of out of the studio to do bits and run up and down the alleyway and things like that."

Upon release, the opening track on *Act of Love*, 'Sing Out, Love Is Easy' received much radio support, but failed to chart. The track's intro section was later turned into a loop and used as the backing theme music for BBC Radio One's weekly chart countdown. A promo video was produced for the new single, but mysteriously disappeared. "I don't know whatever happened to that video," wonders Hirsh today. "But I do recall we did film some footage of that in a swimming bath with Paul swimming."

For bass playing Hook, the lack of success of the second album, combined with having to live off a £50 a week allowance allocated to each band, and having lost interest in the band's music, underscored his decision to leave the band before recording sessions for the third self-titled album began in 1981.

"After the second album we were pretty disillusioned really," admits Hook. "It was again a bit short-sighted of all of us, but we were not experienced in it at all, so Paul and the rest of the band were trying to go in a different direction as if what we've been doing wasn't successful. So, they wanted to make it funkier and jazzier really. And a lot of the songs that they were trying to do didn't appeal to me much and I couldn't get enthusiastic about them. I left by mutual consent really because it just wasn't working for me. I had a son by then and needed to get a proper job and somewhere to live and all the rest of it."

With newcomer Dominic Telfer taking over on bass duties, the group went to work on their third album. Once the self-titled third album was released, the group hit the road supporting ELO on their tour. This would prove to be Voyager's last ever tour, and live the band were augmented by two additional players: a keyboardist/backing vocalist and a guitarist. "In the main we all got on well with each other and there were no serious ego clashes, until we began promoting our third album on tour with ELO," recalls French.

"We used a pianist/backup singer to play some of my parts as I wanted to perform out front more rather than be stuck behind the piano. He shall remain nameless but he had a serious ego problem. Oddly, he remained blissfully unaware of how much we disliked him even though we contrived to steer clear of him when not performing. I must say it was a thrill to be playing big venues such as Wembley Arena and Birmingham NEC even though people hadn't necessarily come to see us. But I do remember there was a lot of after gig partying and celebrating."

"On the tour we brought in Frankie Fish on keys/vocal and Kevin Mann on guitar to expand the sound, originally my idea and on reflection, we could've done without them," admits Hirsh. "Frankie was a good singer, pianist and songwriter who was produced by Gus and managed by Paul Walden. I seem to remember him being a bit crazy and accident prone. Kevin on the other hand responded to an ad in the *Melody Maker* classified ads 'Musicians Wanted 'section. He was a very pleasant chap from the North of England and stayed on with us to help out on some Capital Radio sessions and the final 'write a hit single or you're dropped' recordings ['Like A Stone', 'Good for You' and 'Footprints on The Shore'] as Paul French was under pressure to write a hit to order, which I must say, he did well in these circumstances and stylised them round the synth pop sound of that time.

"I don't recall meeting any of the guys from ELO, although we did see them at sound checks and obviously we saw them at the gigs. Having said that, on the Greg Lake tour we did, Lake's mob weren't that sociable; I don't remember meeting Greg but do remember Gary Moore being a nice chap. They did run a porno movie through the stage auto cues while we were playing on the last night of the tour though!"

With the album struggling to ignite interest or garner any more charting hits, the band were dropped by their label, Mountain Records, who at the same time also went bust. This was another in a line of unfortunate events that the band had to endure.

"We had two experiences of financial problems in our lifetime," affirms Hirsh. "One was when our record producer Gus Dudgeon was robbed by his accountant while we were recording the second album *Act of Love*, and he had to sell his studio. The last thing that he did in his own studio was us, and then he had to sell it. And Jimmy Page bought it. Then Mountain Records went bankrupt. It was probably our fault that they went bankrupt as that's where they lost all their money, then the distribution label RCA took us over, and so that third album came out on RCA."

Undeterred the group soldiered on, releasing a new single 'Like A Stone' b/w 'Good for You' in 1982 which came out via The Flying Record Company, an independent label set up by the band's management. Two more tracks were also recorded at the same recording sessions; 'Footprints on the Shore' and 'Love Not Hollywood'. With 'Life A Stone' failing to garner any interest, the band officially called it a day in 1983.

In 2004, the compilation album *Travels in Time (The Best of The Early Years)* was released on the band's own label Leadhead Records. And then two years later, in 2006, the band reunited, with Chris Hook back on bass, and recorded new material for a fourth album entitled *Eyecontact*, a reference to the 'Halfway Hotel' video. Now an independent entity, the group utilized various non-studio environs for the recording sessions, from guitar parts being recorded in a pub toilet to vocal tracks being recorded in the front room of drummer John Marter's home.

"With *Eyecontact*, we organised that album ourselves," explains Hook. "As, by 2006, you could record stuff on the computer, so we recorded in various places. You didn't need a £10 million recording studio to make an album so that was different for us. We enjoyed doing it and it was done over about a period of a year. It included some songs we had never actually recorded and one of the songs 'Salome' was rescued from a recording we did in the nineties. We rescued that from the master tapes and spruced it up a bit as it was a song that we always thought was great.

"The release of the album was really done by somebody who was working almost part time because he was retired from his job in the music business. It was done a little bit half-heartedly and we didn't really care. We just wanted to do the album. We weren't expecting it to do anything. And I don't think we ever had an expectation of it doing anything apart from the single 'Another Fool' which did get played on prime-time radio. We'd spent a bit more time on that and a bit more time producing it and mastering it and we thought that might do well. It was kind of something to offer the people who were fans who liked Voyager and we sold quite a lot of them on the internet. None of that was through a record company so we set up our own record company."

After twenty years apart, things looked promising again with much belief that a second wind of success was about to blow through. "For a while we really thought we were going to have a breakthrough with 'Another Fool' which was released as the single," says French "We were working very closely with producer Guy Fletcher, who was a big name in the business and
·   who took on the publishing and got very involved in the mix of

the track. He told us he was mates with Terry Wogan's radio show producer who would get behind it. Wogan's show was the most listened to radio slot at the time, but would you believe the producer fell ill with cancer not long before the release date and had to leave the show. Once again, our luck was out!"

French looks back to those halcyon days with much pride and joy. And though he enjoyed every moment of it, both the recording and touring aspects of the business, he is more at home these days in his studio composing and recording production music and classical pieces.

"One thing I can say about touring and gigging generally though is that I don't really miss it at all since retiring," he tells me with a smile. "There was always a pressure to play and perform well in order to grow the fan base and impress someone or other. So, I was always glad to get home to write songs and later compose and score instrumental pieces. That's where I got most satisfaction really and still do."

"It really was about the songs and getting good recordings of the songs," Hirsh says of the band's legacy. "It's all about the studio stuff. In all those years we hardly played live at all, so we never really got on the road and because of that, we didn't develop playing live to the next level. I did a handful of gigs with them before we got the record deal. Then we did that very short UK tour in 1980, then the Greg Lake Tour which was around 10 shows and then ELO which was about 6 shows. So, not very much at all. On reflection, we were too late for prog rock, it was too expensive to tour Australia, up against punk, new wave and disco in the UK, and we should've done the US."

Voyager continues to hold a special place in my musical heart. That moment of hearing the band for the first time on the radio back in 1979 left an indelible mark upon my musical life. One that continues to inform my musical outlook more than forty years later.

****

By 1980 I was in my final year of high school. One Sunday evening I'm sat in front of our television set, as was the ritual every Sunday evening, with my eyes and ears tuned to *Countdown*. A new band is introduced and their new promo video for their song, 'Everybody's Got to Learn Sometime' is aired. A layer of heavy synths create an atmosphere that underscores a emotive, meditative lyric, then lead singer and bass player James Warren stands in a puddle of water as he gentle plucks his bass whilst singing the song. The song floats yet its affirmative message is powerful. The band are called The Korgis, and this is the first time I had heard them.

First released in April of that year, the single finally hit Australia in August and climbed all the way to number 11 on the charts, eventually earning itself the title of the 88th biggest song in Australia that year.

"I remember the director of that video was very in at the time and had done successful videos for some big acts," recalls James Warren today when I asked him about that iconic video. "That video was entirely his concept. We just turned up on the day and he said, 'OK this is what we're going to do, and this is the idea'. And we just went along with it. We were happy and relieved of the possible burden of trying to come up with a whole visual concept. So, we were very glad that it was farmed out to somebody else. It was all shot in a day on a sound stage in London."

Back in 1980, never in my wildest dreams would I have imagined that forty years later I'd end up working with the band, co-writing and recording with them. Life moves in mysterious ways that's for sure. But before I get to that, I need to go back and tell the story of The Korgis.

Prior to forming The Korgis in 1979, Warren and partner Andy Cresswell-Davis were fully fledged members of seventies prog-rock group Stackridge who earned a historic footnote by being the opening act for the very first Glastonbury Festival in 1970. Warren would depart Stackridge in 1974 after the group's third album, the George Martin produced *The Man in*

The Bowler Hat. After Stackridge officially split for the first time in 1976, Davis and Warren would later reunite and form The Korgis a more pop-oriented, synth driven new wave group and were quickly snapped up by Rialto Records.

"Rialto Records was the label set up by two guys Nick and Tim Heath who used to work at EMI Publishing in the UK," explains Warren. "Their father, Ted Heath, had been a very famous band leader during the 1940s in the UK. So, with that background the label, which also started the same year we formed, got off to a great start with The Korgis. We had a song called 'If I Had You', that got to number 13 in the UK charts that same year followed by 'Everybody's Got to Learn Sometime' in 1980 which got to #5 in the UK, was a #1 in France and got to #18 on the Billboard charts in the US so things were really looking up. But I think they were a bit naughty to be honest, because I think they spent a lot of money that they got from The Korgis success on their other acts and probably overspent as their other acts just didn't do anything, so it just went down the tube and so that was the thing that kind of set them on the downward spiral. It just became apparent to us that it just wasn't going to continue working with Rialto. And then that there were various things going on within The Korgis, which made that an unstable entity as well. So, the whole set up became very fragile and it just sort of blew apart after a while."

The Korgis were also happening at a time in musical history which was ripe with creativity, especially with the onset of synthesizers which would come to dominate the eighties. "I was amazed really that we managed to sort of create something because I think there were lots of other acts that we're trying to do the same thing that all fell by the wayside," says Warren. "I mean, maybe it was because we just happened to come up with a couple of really strong songs, which radio loved. We were amazed really because after so many years of trying and getting absolutely nowhere in our previous bands, it suddenly seemed to be more or less overnight where things were transformed for us."

Warren says that the success of 'Everybody's Got to Learn Sometime' brought validation and was a reward for the years he and Davis had spent touring heavily and trying to achieve commercial success in their previous outfit. "I have to say it was an exciting period," he chimes. "I think the biggest world act at the time was probably Blondie. They were making it huge everywhere in Europe especially in the UK. And it was a kind of new thing really because it wasn't exactly punk, even though there were punk elements in Blondie, but it was still kind of melodic pop, but with this great sort of rock edge to it. It was exciting and there were lots of new labels springing up in the UK with acts trying to go down that route of doing a more exciting form of rock with a bit of an edge to it while still being melodic."

While simplicity lies at the heart of 'Everybody's Got to Learn Sometime', the song's chordal structure employs some very complex chord shapes, which raises the musicality of the song to a whole new different level. "I've always been a sucker for tasty chords," says Warren, "and in the late 70s I was increasingly into seeing what I could create on the piano rather than guitar as I was listening to a lot of jazzy stuff and contemporary classical music. I especially liked the way you can spread your fingers on a keyboard and easily come up with strange unexpected changes and clusters. I had a piano in the flat I was living in at the time, and because my ability was very basic, I had to sort of plod along trying to find what I was hearing in my head as I had to translate it into chords on the piano. I still can't play piano as such but about the time of writing 'Everybody's Got to Learn Sometime', I spent many an hour trying to come up with an emotive ballad that had a few of these unexpected clusters.

"And because I love those jazzy bluesy piano type chords, there are a couple of moments in 'Everybody's Got to Learn Sometime' where you do get those kinds of chords. It was also a very deliberate attempt to come up with something incredibly simple because I think simple songs are the hardest to write.

I'd always loved songs like 'Imagine' by John Lennon, for example, which was just so simple yet so powerful. So, with 'Everybody's Got to Learn Sometime', I was trying to come up with something similar to that."

I always wondered why The Korgis never made it down under for a tour, or why they never hit the road to build on the momentum created by the single's success. Warren admits that they were very much a TV orientated project. "We never did a live show or tour because weren't really interested in going out and playing live because Andy Davis, my other partner in The Korgis, when we were in Stackridge, we toured constantly in the UK, and we did hundreds and hundreds of shows and so it was a bit of a relief for us when our label Rialto told us they didn't mind if we were just a studio band. We could just go do TV stuff and radio stuff and make our mark that way. And that suited us down to the ground as we thought we didn't have to go out and tour, we could just stay in the studio and keep writing songs. What could be better than that? And so that was the whole way that we did the project. We just worked on getting TV shows in Europe and maybe the US as well and promoted ourselves that way."

The band were kept informed of the single's success around the world but remained steadfast in their pursuit to break the lucrative American market. "We were so focused on the direction of doing whatever we could to get on the radio in the USA because everyone knew that was where the huge market was at the time," says Warren. "All our energies were funnelled down that route in trying to make it big in the USA. We were very happy to learn that the song got to #1 in France and was doing well in many other territories, but our concentration was entirely on what the hell could we do to get over to the US. Unfortunately, we didn't do any major shows in the USA. We did lots of TV and radio promotion over there and we went over to LA and to New York and that was fun. It was great fun. We did a lot of the smaller sort of the channels that we were on. But, regardless, the record still broke through and ended up getting to #18 on the Billboard Hot 100 which was a great result."

While 'Everybody's Got to Learn Sometime' and its parent album, *Dumb Waiters,* finally delivered the group their much-needed breakthrough on a global scale, it hadn't come without a cost. The recording sessions for *Dumb Waiters* were fraught with much difficulty, and inner tensions frayed to the point that Davis departed the group midway through recording, leaving the group a man down, and forcing Warren to pick up the pieces and soldier on.

"Andy and I always had a fractious relationship," reveals Warren. "We were as different as chalk and cheese as people and after a while, we would just piss each other off completely. The straw that broke the camel's back with Andy and I in the *Dumb Waiters* period was our differing arrangement and production approaches: I was always keen to add more vocal harmonies and go to the lush end of the production spectrum whereas Andy was all for keeping it raw and relatively unproduced. So one day he suddenly announced he'd had enough and was gone. But actually, even though our obvious musical and personality differences were never going to ensure a positive working situation, there was another, probably more significant undercurrent at play which resulted in Andy's abrupt walkout: he couldn't cope with success — and all the pressure, demands and expectations that come with it. So, there we were in the studio trying to complete the *Dumb Waiters* project, with the record label urging us to come up with some more radio-friendly tunes to follow in the footsteps of 'If I Had You', and Andy hits the self-destruct button at the worst possible moment and abandons the project. He didn't participate in any of the promo for the album after that, nor the video for 'Everybody's Got to Learn Sometime'.

"Andy did the same thing in the Stackridge era. We'd just finished working with George Martin on *The Man in The Bowler Hat* album and, at that critical moment, when we could have consolidated on the commercial progress, Andy fomented a split in the band and basically threw away all we'd achieved. It must be some sort of deep-seated neurosis about success and entitlement, I guess. As we all know, groups are a classic breeding ground for this sort of thing."

With Davis now gone, Warren had to re-sing the material that he originally meant to have been by Davis, which for Warren required him adjusting his vocal range to match Davis voice which was in a lower register.

"Songs such as 'Perfect Hostess' is an example of a song that Andy was meant to sing," expounds Warren. "In fact, it was recorded with him singing before he walked out so I had to re-record it because I was the only one left in the band, so to speak. And in those days, you couldn't just easily retune a track to whatever key you wanted to do it in. It was what it was and you had to match your voice to it. It was not wholly satisfying for me personally for that reason. I didn't like my voice on some of those songs."

The group persevered, eventually recording and releasing the follow-up album, *Sticky George*, in 1981. In due course matters continued to splinter, causing the group to implode in 1983 which also led to the closure of Rialto Records as well.

Now adrift in a sea of uncertainty, with feelings of insecurity underscoring his resolve, Warren decided to move forward as a solo artist. "I thought that maybe I could do it," he says, "so, I started writing as many songs as I could and thinking of my future as being more of a solo artist, but being with a group of people is really what I enjoy most. I didn't really like the idea of just being sat in my own bedroom, trying to come up with songs all the time and just being a lonely sort of musician again, like I was when I was 16. So, groups have always been where it's been at for me. I didn't quite know how to how to go forward after the original line-up came to an end, so it was a bit of a strange time for me, and a bit of a confusing period."

While Warren was navigating his way through the wreckage of the band's split, and trying to find his feet again, he was unaware that in Brazil one of his songs had just been picked up by a popular television soap opera *Sol de Verão*, (English translation is 'The Summer Sun') which ran from October 1982 to March 1983, bringing a much-needed boost to his self-confidence.

"I had this ballad called 'Don't Look Back', that I recorded with Trevor Horn, who was a really successful producer at the time and though he did a good job with it, looking back on it, I'm kind of disappointed because I think I tried to interfere too much in what he was doing. I really wish I'd just said, 'OK, here's the song and just do whatever you like'. I think the result may have been stronger because even though I think what we did was very good, and it's a good song, we could have had much more success had I just let him do whatever he wanted. So, it didn't make it in the UK because of that.

"Amazingly in Brazil the producers of a daytime TV soap that was on like three or four days a week in the mornings on one of their major channels, picked up on the song and used it to start and end the show. And so people just loved it over there and we still get fan mail now from Brazilian people saying, 'when are you going to come to Brazil, because we just love that song'. So they talk about *that* song there and not 'Everybody's Got to Learn Sometime'. It was a complete fluke as we had no idea that the song had been played over there until we got news of it having this kind of success."

By the 1990s the musical climate had change considerably, with grunge now the dominating musical force of the day. It's more earthy and darker elements connecting with a generation of disenchanted youth. By contrast the lighter and more uplifting sounds of pop still resonated with those of an era where The Beatles and The Beach Boys were the soundtrack of their youth. Ever the optimist, Warren concocted an idea of finally putting together a new line-up of the band for some live performances. Enter Al Steele, guitarist extraordinaire and creative spark who would prove to be the missing link for Warren.

"We first met Al in the 1990s when myself and John Baker

[guitar and keyboards], my old friend who became a sort of a permanent Korgi with me in the early 1980s," chimes Warren. "So, come about 1990 we had this idea that maybe we could do some live shows. We asked people if they knew of a good guitar player or a good keyboard player and we got a few people involved and then a friend of ours told us about a great guitarist who was positive and upbeat called Al Steele. So, he came over to where we live in Bath, England for an audition, and was exactly that. And so, we rehearsed and did a few shows with Al, but it didn't come to much after that."

The story of The Korgis may have ended there, if not for a turn of events in 2015. With a reappraisal of the band's legacy, and with Steele re-entering the picture, the future of The Korgis and their present status was finally etched in stone. "We reconnected with Al again and went down to his studio, Shabbey Road Studios near Cardiff in Wales, and he was the same as ever, still as positive, and as fun as he was when we first met him. But what I didn't realise when we first met him was that he was an incredible creative musician as well. I thought he was just like a guitar for hire kind of musician. He can write great songs and words and do all the orchestral arrangements that go with them. He's just sensational and he really made everything happen for us."

After forty years, I finally got to meet Warren, via the wonders of technology, and did a Zoom interview with him in 2021 for a feature story I was writing on The Korgis for popular American music magazine *Goldmine*. The quietly spoken Warren exuded a youthful demure, his passion for song-writing and music still burning brightly. His thoughtful responses, and openness was refreshing. After expounding on the art of song-writing, I mentioned my own music to him and how I had some musical ideas lying around that might make for a good collaboration with his band. He asked me to send through some of my material. The idea spawned our first collaboration, titled 'Always A Sunny Day', a slice of heavenly pop melodicism that blended perfectly with his style. Much to my surprise, and in a synchronous moment, I later found out Steele had spent his childhood in Shepparton, where I had resided for many years. Sometimes life can definitely be stranger than fiction.

Over the past few years the band have kept up a busy schedule of live shows in their native England. For many fans of the band, seeing the band finally perform live is welcomed and much overdue. "Everyone says to us it's great to see you back, as it's been such a long time since you've been on the road," laughs Warren. "And we remind them that this current period of the band is the first time that we've actually been a live band. It is surprising, as not many people will like us in that respect. Bands like The Buggles also just concentrated entirely on TV and radio, and it worked for them. And we were in that little bubble too and we really enjoyed it."

Since the initial collaboration, the band and I have worked on two more songs, 'Red Flag Day' and 'Letter to Geelong'. What makes a good pop song great is that they will pass the test of time, and 'Everybody's Got to Learn Sometime' is one of those tunes. The song is a hugely popular as a choice cover, with many artists ranging from Italian pop singer Zucchero to English synth pop-sters Erasure, to American alt-rocker Beck whose cover appeared in the 2004 film, *Eternal Sunshine of the Spotless Mind*, all recording their own take on the song.

I have always wondered why certain songs will connect with an audience, while others fall by the wayside. In this particular case, what attracted me to The Korgis was their unique mix of quirkiness, and their elegant, ethereal approach to crafting pop songs. Also, the song's more introspective lyrical matter that leaned towards Buddhist philosophy was another point of particular note. One can't overlook the huge influence of The Beatles too, as it shines through in spades. But then again, what band on this planet doesn't owe something, no matter how miniscule, to The Beatles?

At the end of the day, the song left its mark upon me. Its synth-based sound, with not a guitar in sight, opened my ears to other instruments, and a different way to paint a sonic canvas using a multitude of aural colours to achieve a different effect. Both Voyager and The Korgis, and to a larger extent Freddie Mercury's piano playing on Queen's 'Bohemian Rhapsody', aroused an interest in me wanting to learn to play a secondary instrument, the piano, though at a rather rudimentary level, but enough to be able to add touches of keys on my own recordings.

'Everybody's Got to Learn Sometime' is another in a long list of songs that shaped my musical vocabulary and knowledge. Another piece of the jigsaw to my musical life.

9: City To City

It's early 1978 and the new single by Scottish singer-songwriter Gerry Rafferty, 'Baker Street', is blasting out of my small transistor AM radio. The hypnotic sax hook, lyrical content, musical arrangement and the voice engulfs me, striking a chord deep within my soul. This is music coming truly from the heart. It sweeps me away from my teenage existence into another world, a world so far away. And I'm hooked, big time. I hit the local record store and buy the 7-inch single and, later, the album it came from, *City to City*. It went on to become one of my favourite albums and over the ensuing years provided a soundtrack to my life. Later, it inspired my own songwriting and approach to making music.

Once I had the album, I realized that the song as I first heard on my radio was actually an abridged cut, edited from the six-minute-long album version to make it much friendlier to radio playlists where a three-and-a-half-minute song was considered ideal, though when it came to FM radio, longer tracks and album cuts better suited the format. There had been long songs that had been accepted by radio such as Led Zeppelin's 'Stairway to Heaven' which ran to over seven minutes, and Queen's 'Bohemian Rhapsody', which clocked just under six minutes, but they were the exceptions to the rule.

The promotional video for 'Baker Street', made in the pre-MTV era, begins slowly, focussing on a view of a street parking meter, as a Mini Moog, playing a flute-like refrain, launches the song. This parking metre occupies a space in front of a road sign that clearly states 'Baker Street W1', a busy thoroughfare in the heart of the swanky Marylebone district of London, about two miles from central London, and the fictional home to Sherlock Holmes. I made a pilgrimage to Baker Street on many occasions, and walked the street with the words of the song running through my head, envisaging the imagery described by Rafferty in his song. It gave me a better understanding of the subject matter and captured the spirit Rafferty intended.

The next scene in the video switched to Rafferty and his band performing the song in the dimly lit surrounds of a recording studio and as the signature sax riff kicks in, the pans out as a smoke machine, giving the illusion of fog filtering through the studio, brings an atmospheric touch to proceedings, that perfectly underscores the haunting melody. As the footage moves forward, we get a close-up shot of Rafferty as he begins singing the first lines of the song. In another later shot, we get a brief glimpse of the street, showing people going about their business, emphasizing the moving and yearning theme of the song's melancholic subject matter. As the song reaches its sonic crowning point, the high-octane guitar solo lifts off, and we get yet another glimpse of the street. Another important facet of 'Baker Street' was the saxophone sounds which made it stand out among the guitar-led new wave and post-punk songs of the day. Once the song picked up speed with radio programmers everywhere, it became inescapable. It was everywhere. And deservedly so.

****

Looking back more than 45-plus years later, I view *City to City* as one of the quintessential albums of all time, on an equal footing for me as The Beatles' *Sgt. Pepper's Lonely Hearts Club Band*, The Beach Boys' *Pet Sounds* and Pink Floyd's *The Dark Side of the Moon*. While Rafferty went on to write and record further exemplary music, the immense commercial success of *City to City*, and 'Baker Street', overshadowed everything else he did. It is the one album that will forever be attached to his legacy, it is his signature work, and the tune that firmly secured his place in music history.

I've worn out numerous copies over the years: vinyl,

cassettes, CDs, and each time I've bought a replacement. So much so, that I've even, over time, collected numerous pressings of the same album on vinyl from various countries around the world from Germany to Sweden and beyond, spending my free hours on tour seeking out second-hand record stores and thrift stores in a quest to find another pressing. I have limited edition blue and red vinyl pressings. I have pressings that were issued with incorrect track listings. The list is endless. Call it a passion or, maybe an obsession.

So what is it about this album, and Rafferty in particular, that casts such an enormous pull over my life? Let's start with the man himself. A gifted songwriter whose lyrics were infused with an emotional depth that sprang from the depths of his soul, much of Rafferty's writing was inspired by his enormous love for his family, evident in some of the songs on *City to City*, in particular 'Mattie's Rag', which was written for his daughter Martha, and 'Right Down the Line' written for his then wife.

A sense of family, connectedness and a longing for home were at the core of Rafferty's song-writing spirit. Born in Paisley, about ten miles from Glasgow, Rafferty was, and always remained, a true Scotsman at heart, with a deep love for his family and country. His frequent travels to and experiences in London also provided much song-writing inspiration as was highlighted on 'Baker Street', while his Scottish roots were echoed in 'The Ark'. These are all universal themes that everyone can relate to, themes which form the basis of many other timeless classics.

Then there is the music which, from a musician's point of view, is superbly crafted. Every element came together at the precise moment, brick by brick, building its sonic framework to perfection, so that it could convey its aural message to the listener. The melodies soar and are memorable. The songs get inside you, and never leave. It is popular music at its finest. Not the sort that is subject to the latest trend of the day, that later becomes a throwaway, it is music that transcends a contemporary time frame and continues to sound fresh decades on, its message still resonating after all these years. This is the mark of a true musical genius.

And the album's most famous song, the resplendent 'Baker Street', with its iconic signature sax motif, is a textbook lesson in song-writing itself. The song's emotionally-charged lyrics underscore the alienation of city life while at the same, reflecting a desire and longing for home. Then there is the subtle use of "slash" chords — for the musically uninitiated, these are chords that imply a second related chord by the use of a bass note, for example A/D. In this case, A is the primary chord, while the D note in the bass gives the illusion of another chord D being heard whilst providing a moving bass line, especially when used by piano and guitar. Its use here perfectly suits the travelling aspect to the song's lyrical content: "Winding your way down on Baker Street." It brings to the song and music a sophisticated edge and shows the depth and knowledge of Rafferty's musicianship and song-writing genius. Add to that the searing guitar solo played by Hugh Burns which is held in high regard by many guitarists due to its strong melodic content and is instantly recognizable.

****

Prior to making *City to City* Rafferty spent several years amid much legal wrangling and personal turmoil with his former record label in the aftermath of the demise of his band Stealers Wheel who had topped the charts with 'Stuck in the Middle with You' in 1973. Before this, Rafferty had also recorded a debut solo album, *Can I Have My Money Back?* (1971) which itself came in the aftermath of the breakup of his folk-rock combo The Humblebums that featured famed comedian Billy Connolly in its line-up. Yet it was during this tumultuous three-year period that Rafferty would begin assembling the material that gave birth to *City to City*.

"*City to City* came on the back of an admirable body of work by Gerry," explains Rafferty's elder brother Jim, "following that with Joe Egan in Stealers Wheel, reinforced in the opinion of those who had followed his work over the previous years that here was no flash in the pan, but a singer and writer of singular gifts operating at the peak of his powers, and with still more to give."

Former manager Jon Brewer, who had previously worked with artists such as David Bowie and Gene Clark of The Byrds, took a gamble on Rafferty after hearing the demos of *City to City*, which Rafferty had recorded on his four-track Teac machine at his home. "On those tapes there were two tracks that stood out, one called 'City to City' and the other 'Baker Street'," Brewer recalls. "Eventually I was asked if I would manage or fund a new album based on some demos that had been recorded. I agreed to do so and put together not a management agreement but a production agreement to produce three records."

Rafferty signed to United Artists but before work began on *City To City*, he took on the task of producing seven out of the ten tracks on his brother Jim's debut album, *Don't Talk Back*. "Gerry, never having been in the producer's chair before, was probably a little apprehensive concerning the responsibility for the efficiency and smooth running of the production," recalls Jim, "and so recruited an old ally, Mike Day, a recording engineer who had been responsible for assisting Gerry in the recording of four track demos of his songs, many of which would be later re-recorded for *City to City*.

"Mike was a capable pair of hands throughout the making of *Don't Talk Back* and eased Gerry over any technical hurdles he encountered in the production and the finished article turned out to be as polished and professional an artefact as anyone could have wished, as well as being thoroughly enjoyable and memorable for everyone who took part. It was a particular feature of this album that Gerry and I got to sing together, providing the harmony vocals which were a prominent part of the process."

With his brother's album now completed Gerry, with producer Hugh Murphy by his side, entered Chipping Norton studios in England in the summer of 1977 with a handful of demos that included a version of 'Baker Street', which featured Rafferty playing the melody of the now iconic sax intro on guitar, contrary to the claims made later by Raphael Ravenscroft who played the sax on the track, of him having written it himself.

"Raf did not come up with it," confirms Gary Taylor, who played bass guitar on the album and who first worked with Rafferty on *Can I Have My Money Back?*, "He did a brilliant job of it, but Gerry had that riff right from the start. It was already on the demo Gerry played me prior to assembling the band that went into the studio to record the album." When *City to City* was reissued on CD in 2011 it included that very demo of 'Baker Street', proving once and for all that it already existed way before Ravenscroft was hired to play the part and forever putting the dispute to bed.

Rafferty assembled the material for the album, with his demoed songs forming the basis for the album. He also brought in an unfinished track — 'The Ark' — which dated back to 1970, around the time Rafferty was working on his first solo album — it is a Celtic-infused track which opens the album and was also the first track that recording sessions for the album began with.

Rafferty's daughter Martha recalls how much of the material had been hibernating for many years in one form or another. "He would work on songs over years, sometimes decades," she reveals. "He'd have many melodies, or a line or two in his back pocket, and he'd wait until it seemed the right time to use them. I remember all the songs on *City to City* being written and developing organically over a number of years. He had a home studio and would spend every day playing. The lyrics always came later and were the hardest part for him. Inspiration would come when he was alone, normally late at night. I remember hearing the tracks when we'd be driving around Glasgow in the car and always had a sense that there was a touch of magic in those songs. At his best there has always been a connection to the mystical or a window to the great unknown, a transcendence of the ordinary. That's what all great art is about and that's what he wanted his work to convey, that life is ultimately meaningful and beautiful."

Back in the studio, two weeks were spent on recording the basic tracks for the album which comprised Tommy Eyre on piano, Gary Taylor on Bass, Henry Spinetti on drums, and guitarist Hugh Burns, while Rafferty set himself up in a little sound booth singing the songs which the band played along to. Both Burns and Spinetti had been hired by Rafferty after he had produced seven of the tracks (and provided backing vocals as well) to his brother Jim's debut album.

"A lot of the lyrics hadn't been written yet," recalls Taylor about the *City to City* recording sessions. "He had a lot of ideas of how he wanted the songs to go but, basically, we got free reign to do what we wanted to do. And if he didn't like something or wanted to change something, he'd make suggestions. And certainly, when we did the 'Baker Street' track, Gerry just sang the sax riff or what turned out to be the sax riff because at that time, no one had any idea what was actually going to play that. But from a musical point of view, I thought he was great to work with. And every time he played you a new song, the hairs on the back of your neck went up, because he was brilliant as a writer. He was the most amazing artist I have ever worked with."

Rafferty also brought in multi-instrumentalist and arranger Graham Preskett to add fiddle, mandolin and keyboards to some of the album's material as well as undertake arranging of the material. "I tracked lots of fiddles — and some mandolin — on 'The Ark', 'City to City' and I sang along with the fiddle in the intro, 'woo-woohing' which he liked enough to keep in, and 'Waiting for the Day'," Preskett says, "he seemed impressed by how quickly I tracked, so asked me to do real string arrangements for 'Baker Street', 'Home and Dry', 'Stealin' Time' and 'Mattie's Rag', plus a New Orleans style marching band for 'Mattie's Rag'. I worked hard on the arrangements for strings and that song but had loads of other stuff on at the same time and fell asleep writing out the parts the night before. I woke up and had to get my then-wife to drive me from London to Chipping Norton, most of the time behind a slow lorry. I was frantically writing out string, brass and wind parts in the car! On arrival I found that only half the marching-band I asked for had been booked. I believe we had to track the different parts and it was difficult for Gerry to imagine what it was going to sound like. We finished late, and I still hadn't finished all the string parts for the afternoon session. I was not feeling good at this point!

"Because of the morning's overrun, we started the afternoon string session late. 'Baker Street' and 'Home and Dry' went very well, but I had to promise Gerry that I would use my string machine for 'Mattie's Rag' and 'Stealin' Time'. Thankfully, these also went well and I added the arpeggio effects in the verse of 'Baker Street', plus a tracked folk/jazzy solo in 'Mattie's Rag', which mirrored the natty clarinet part I had written for Gerry's interesting chords. All in all, it was a pleasure working for him and he thought well enough of my efforts to book me on mandolin, fiddle, arranging and keyboards his following album, *Night Owl*."

While the bulk of the album was recorded at Chipping Norton, several additional sessions were also undertaken at Marquee Studios and Berwick Street Studios. Once recording was completed, it went off to mixing.

"We mixed *City to City* over a two-week period in Sept/Oct 1977 in studio two at Advision Studios in London," remembers Declan O'Doherty, the mix engineer on *City to City*. "The console had automated mixdown, but producer Hugh Murphy was not a fan and all the mixes were done manually. Hugh had an upbeat and outgoing personality, while Gerry was a bit quieter — though he had a keen sense of humour. I liked them both. The atmosphere was one of friendly collaboration and camaraderie.

"I was particularly struck by Gerry's voice and vocal

technique. He also seemed able to accurately double track his performances in one take, which was impressive. Some of the songs were densely arranged and orchestrated. Hugh and Gerry were very much 'hands on'. Getting each mix just right required hours of listening and fine tuning. The studio was comfortable and quiet with few interruptions. Although the mix sessions were long and required intense concentration, there were many lighter moments too — with a few coffee and sandwich breaks here and there. The songs would remain firmly stuck in my head for months.

"At the time, I was not aware of Gerry's battles with the music industry, nor did I know anything about his personal life. We focused on the job at hand and got it done to everyone's satisfaction. In some ways it was a spiritual and quite overwhelming experience. That probably had a lot to do with the songs and lyrics and the effect they had on me. It was all about tapping into the power of those songs/arrangements and capturing the ebb and flow of emotions in them. For me, it was a ground-breaking and pivotal moment in my career."

The album was finally completed in late 1977 at a cost of £18,000. Featuring artwork by fellow Scot, artist and playwright John Patrick Byrne, (who had previously done art for The Beatles, Donovan and Stealers Wheel), *City to City* was finally released on January 20, 1978. Six of its tracks were released as singles, though in the US, United Artists only issued three singles, 'Baker Street', 'Right Down The Line' and 'Home and Dry', with all three bona-fide Top 40 hits.

The first cab off the rank in the US was 'Baker Street', though United Artists initially had no plans to release the track as a single, as in the UK 'City to City' had been released as the first single and failed to set the chart alight, though it found success in the Netherlands where Rafferty was invited by Dutch weekly pop music TV show *TopPop* to perform on the proviso that he be accompanied by Hugh Murphy who co-produced the album. Rafferty's performance, which aired in February 1978, saw Murphy miming the playing of a harmonica which on the recorded version was played by Paul Jones, former singer with Manfred Mann.

"The producer of the album, Hugh Murphy, is probably the person who hauled me into the project," Jones recalled, "Hugh had said that in his early days he ran our (Manfred Mann) fan club; I don't remember much about that, but he certainly was around, and continued to be for quite a considerable time. I recall that our paths crossed now and again after his direct association with The Manfreds ended. So, he would have known that I played harmonica, and if anyone had said 'it's a train song — it must have a harmonica', that would be when I got the call. Though I have no recollection of being in Chipping Norton Studios with that amazing collection of musicians so I cannot be sure that I was at the session for this track. It was a common occurrence for my harmonica to be subsequently overdubbed in those days and seeing that Marquee, and Berwick Street Studios were credited on the sleeve of the record, I would guess that's where my contribution was added."

'Baker Street' would change Rafferty's fortunes, not only in the UK but worldwide. After much passionate persuasion by Rafferty, the label went ahead and released the song on February 3 1978. It would peak at No. 2 in the US, spending six weeks in that position on Billboard's Hot 100 in the later part of June 1978, and was only held off from the top spot by Andy Gibb's 'Shadow Dancing'.

To cause further frustration, Billboard's rival *Cashbox* magazine had its own weekly Top 100 singles chart which had the top two positions reversed: 'Baker Street' was at No. 1 for two weeks in July 1978, while 'Shadow Dancing' was at No. 2. 'Right Down the Line' was issued as the follow-up single and peaked at No. 12 in October before a third and final single, 'Home and Dry' peaked at No. 28 in February 1979.

'Right Down the Line' is another personal favourite of mine on *City To City*. The song's subject matter of love, devotion and trust in a relationship eloquently affirms Rafferty love for his wife Carla Ventilla. The words flow with soulful sentiment, as

Rafferty sings the lilting melody with a tenderness that soothes and caresses. It is a timeless ballad oozing with authenticity, inducing the listener to pause and reflect. It is a song that never comes off sounding cheesy or overtly saccharine, it speaks directly to the heart leaving you without any shadow of a doubt to the conviction and love Rafferty had for his wife which 'Right Down the Line' affirms in abundance.

It was via this song that I first expressed my love to my wife Liz. At the time, she had not heard much of Gerry Rafferty's music apart from 'Baker Street', but she became a convert immediately after hearing this song. I grabbed the CD version, placed into the CD player, and we listened together as we sat quietly in the room of the shared house I was living in at the time. The words perfectly encapsulated what I wanted to express to her. It later inspired me to write my own musical love letter to my wife, writing my song 'Shining Star' for her.

Just like 'Baker Street', 'Right Down The Line' is another fine example of Rafferty's song-writing finesse. It is a cleverly-crafted song and rather than incorporating a separate chord progression for the verse and chorus as is the norm for many songs, it takes a different route, using the same chord progression throughout. At its core, it is primarily a two-part structured arrangement; one part verse, with the "right down the line" alluding to a chorus at the tail end of each, and one part bridge in the "I just want to say…" line. And yet again, it radiates sophistication. The tonality of D minor dominates the verse sections while in the bridge sections it switches to D major, causing the shift in keys from the more poignant and sombre colour of the minor key to the more uplifting and hopeful colour of the major key. And the sparse instrumentation in the minor section further emphasizes the lyrical nature of the verses as the mood lifts for the affirmation in the bridge, additional instrumentation drives home the message.

City to City would go on to sell five and a half million copies and top the Billboard charts, finally removing the *Saturday Night Fever* soundtrack from the No. 1 position in July 1978. The label expected Rafferty to tour in support of the album and build upon the momentum, but he refused to tour America.

"There were very few dates which Gerry did and that was one of the reasons why we did not see eye to eye," remembers Brewer. "He wanted to do *The David Frost Show* in the U.S. and he just had success with 'Baker Street' in the U.S. I told him that he should not do it as I was concerned that his career would be over, especially when I found out what he was going to say. He was going to tell everyone that he was not going to tour and knowing American audiences that would probably kill his career. He did do the show, and I think his career went downhill from then because of it."

Jim Rafferty categorically disputes Brewer's account. "Brewer's assertion that Gerry's career went downhill as a result of his disinclination to tour America is a glaring misinterpretation," he affirms. "A number of factors were in play, which brought a gradual decline in his musical profile, which would included changes of fashion in musical styles and demographics, the rise of digital downloads, plus his disaffection with new methods of creating and distributing music."

Much has been written over the years regarding Rafferty's supposed aversion to fame and fortune, and is largely based on hearsay and innuendo. Jim Rafferty sets the record straight. "Gerry did not dislike the success he enjoyed from the popularity of his work," he explains. "Like most people he relished the improvement in lifestyle and the advantages it brought his way as a result — plus the ability to turn down any offer which he felt inappropriate or in any way conflicting with the manner in which he wanted to live his life, that this included a distaste for the promotional requirements of record companies, the wishes of management is well known to anyone who has read the numerous interviews he gave on the subject. In short, he took the view that he had more than paid his debt to the record companies whom he was signed to at varying points in his musical trajectory, by virtue of sales of his music."

"Brewer's claims are all nonsense," concurs his daughter,

Martha, "(Gerry) would come to the U.S. to do some press and was catapulted into the celebrity scene with parties, limos, drugs, and all of that. He decided then it was too far removed from who and what he stood for, so he walked away. He enjoyed live performances and always had a great deal of respect for his fans. It was the machinations around the music business that he had a healthy distrust of."

In an interview with BBC Radio 2 in September 2000, Gerry explained the reasoning behind his decision not to tour. "It was something I was fiercely protective of in myself. Because I knew in the long term, 20 or 30 years on, I wanted to still be making music and not to become a name of a famous musician or of a celebrity which would have overtaken the music, and which has happened to many, many people and continues to do so today."

At the 1978 Grammy Awards, Rafferty earned two nominations for 'Baker Street' in the form of Record of the Year and Best Pop Vocal Performance. The song also won him two Ivor Novello awards. And it's been rumoured that 'Baker Street' has earned Rafferty a cool £80,000 per year since its release in 1978.

****

Rafferty followed up *City To City* with *Night Owl* released in June 1979, an album that build upon its predecessor both musically and lyrically, with the album also meeting with much success, though falling short of its predecessor's commercial heights. While the title track was issued as the lead single from the album for the UK, in the US 'Days Gone Down (Still Got the Light in Your Eyes)' was used instead. The album also featured the track 'Take the Money and Run', which was originally slated for *City To City* but Rafferty didn't feel it was right for that album and so held it over until *Night Owl*.

It was also during the recording sessions for *Night Owl* that Taylor got to experience the type of pressure Rafferty was under, with tensions leading to Taylor's dismissal. "We had begun making the *Night Owl* album and had been working for about four days," recalls Taylor, "and we'd done 'Get It Right Next Time' and were working on one other track. Gerry had been in the control room when suddenly he walked into the studio and just said, 'I can't stand it anymore' and walked out! And that was the end of my and Tommy Eyre's tenure with Gerry as we learned a couple days later that we had been fired. And I never saw Gerry again and never found out why. It was mystifying."

With *Night Owl* completed, Rafferty also took time out to handle production duties for a new album by husband-and-wife folk-rock duo Richard and Linda Thompson. But recording sessions were fraught with tension and upon completion of the album and with no interest from record labels, it was shelved. Though the duo would later re-record the album with a new producer behind the desk, it was eventually released in 1982 under the title of *Shoot Out the Lights.*

Having followed a musical formula somewhat with *City To City*, *Night Owl* and *Snakes And Ladders*, for his next album, *Sleepwalking* (1982), Rafferty ventured down a very different route where he introduced synthesizers and drum machines into the mix and at the suggestion of his label, also brought in a new producer, Christopher Neil. The album would also feature two members from the band Dire Straits: keyboardist Alan Clark and drummer Pick Withers on several tracks.

"He was a joy to work with and accepted what I conjured up happily," recalls Clark on his time working with Rafferty in the studio. "However the co-producer on *Sleepwalking*, Christopher Neil, was a bit of a pain in so much as he seemed to constantly have a different opinion. But we got there!"

"Gerry did not enjoy working with him, due no doubt to Neil having ideas of his own," concurs Jim Rafferty. Due to Clark's involvement on the album, Rafferty would later return the favour and contribute lead vocals to the track 'The Way It Always Starts' that appeared on Mark Knopfler's soundtrack album *Local Hero*. With *Sleepwalking* not meeting commercial expectations, Gerry was dropped by his label and in its aftermath, took a six-year hiatus. During this break he built his own recording studio in his home and toiled away working on his own, and at times with Hugh Murphy, at his own pace. In 1987, he produced the single 'Letter from America' for fellow Scots The Proclaimers which would peak at #3 on the UK charts.

"The Proclaimers had just signed a deal with an independent label and the label sent Gerry a few of their songs," remembers Alan Rafferty. "'Letter From America' stood out to Gerry and, as a fellow Scot, he could relate to the lyrics, so moved them into his home at Tye Farm for a few days and recorded the track there. He is hidden in the mix on backing vocals as well, on the last chorus."

The following year saw Rafferty return with his sixth album, *North and South*, a record that contained a diverse number of styles and confirmed Rafferty's evolution as a musician and songwriter. Though the material was strong and solid and his best work since *City To City*, only one single was issued, 'Shipyard Town', that only confirmed Rafferty's commercial decline.

In 1992, Stealers Wheel's 'Stuck In The Middle With You' was used in a pivotal scene in Quentin Tarantino's classic movie, *Reservoir Dogs* introducing the song, and Rafferty, to a whole new generation of music fans. That same year his next album *On a Wing & a Prayer* appeared with little fanfare. The album featured three co-writes with brother Jim (who also provided backing vocals on several tracks) and a reunion with his old Stealers Wheel musical partner Joe Egan who also provided backing vocals.

Rafferty embarked on a rare major European tour in February 1993 that would take in dates in Germany, Belgium, England and Scotland in support of his *On a Wing and a Prayer* album. But on the first date of the tour, in Hamburg, Germany, he got laryngitis. He soldiered on with the rest of the German dates and Belgian date until he got to the Edinburgh Playhouse show — which was also recorded by BBC Radio — where he was visibly struggling. The next day his doctor ordered the cancellation of the last two gigs of the tour in Glasgow and London. Both would be rescheduled in early March. He performed his last show of the tour and his last ever live performance, on March 4, 1993 at London's Hammersmith Apollo. The band that backed Rafferty at the last show consisted of; Liam Genockey on drums, Pete Zorn on bass, Hugh Burns and Jerry Donahue on guitars, Kenny Craddock and Pavel Rosak on keyboards, Liane Carroll also on keyboards and backing vocals, Arran Amun on percussion, Mel Collins on saxophone and Nicky Moore on backing vocals.

In 1994, his next album *Over My Head* featured a combination of new and reworked material along with a couple of covers, one of which was John Lennon's 'Out of the Blue', but was largely ignored. By the time of 2000's *Another World* — which was only made available via Rafferty's website — he was at a nadir. "Gerry had just been through a tumultuous decade," explains Alan Rafferty. "He'd been divorced, lost his mother and eldest brother, Joe. His descent into alcoholism had gathered pace and for the first time it showed in the quality of the writing and production of the songs. It seemed he had lost that wonderful ability to capture the nuances of life and relationships, as he had done on all his previous albums. This album was largely fictional, lyrically speaking and none of the songs on it were anywhere near his usual standard. It's the one album by Gerry that I can't relate to and never listen to. It didn't just damage his finances — it cost £200,000 to produce — it also seriously damaged his musical legacy in my opinion. By that point, the only people around him were 'Yes men', when what he needed was a friend to take him aside and have a word."

The album saw Mark Knopfler returning the favour to Rafferty, by contributing guitar throughout. His next album appeared in 2009 in the form of *Life Goes On*, a more personal outing that featured a mixture of six new songs, reworked older tracks from previous albums, a selection of Christmas carols and a couple of choice covers.

When Gerry Rafferty passed away on January 4, 2011, he was 63 and the world lost a true musical legend. Over the years Rafferty's enormous influence has been acknowledged by many, and the various cover versions of 'Baker Street' which attest to the man's brilliance and ongoing influence.

On the tenth anniversary of his death, a posthumous final album was issued. Entitled *Rest In Blue* and compiled by his daughter Martha, it featured an array of material previously demoed, from various stages of Rafferty's career, some dating as far back to 1970. Stripped back to just Rafferty's vocals, musicians who had worked with Rafferty over the course of his career were brought in and cobbled together the material in new recordings providing a fitting tribute to one of Scotland's most beloved songwriters.

Rafferty's music lives on and continues to resonate with audiences decades later as was evident when 'Right Down The Line' was given a new lease of life in 2022 after it was featured in several American television series; *Euphoria*, *Ozark* and *Shining Girls*, it introduced the song — and Rafferty — to a whole new generation of music fans.

I wrote an early abridged version of this chapter which was published as 'Cherishing the Gerry Rafferty album City To City' in the April 2021 issue of Goldmine magazine.

10: The Kids Wanna Rock

I'd just turned eighteen when I first heard a young Canadian rocker named Bryan Adams through his just released single 'Cuts Like a Knife', which I happened to hear one day on an Australian FM radio station during a visit to the city from my country home. Commercial FM radio had only arrived in Australia a few short years prior in the major cities, while in the regional centres, it was yet to make its presence, with AM radio still the dominant broadcasting platform.

The song captured my attention in all its glory; the guitar, the voice, the sound, it was all to my liking. I later found out it was the title song from his new album that had been recently released. I immediately went out and purchased a copy and it instantly resonated with me. The album's cover featured a blond-haired Adams dressed in a black leather jacket, tight fitting denim jeans, and baseball boots. He is holding a Rickenbacker guitar in one hand and the way he poses in the image, it looks as if he has been caught in the act and about to make a run for it. It's a very cool image. The flip-side of the cover saw Adams with a cheeky look on his face further highlighting the, "uh-oh, you caught me out" pose. The album became a staple on my turntable. In fact, I liked it so much I bought a cassette version so that I didn't wear out my vinyl copy and could listen to it on my car stereo.

I remember flicking through a music magazine at the time and seeing a very clever promotional ad for the album, which read, "Bryan Adams Cuts Like A Knife...And the Cut is Getting Deeper". I loved the play on words. To me, *Cuts Like a Knife* signposted what was to come on *Reckless*, featuring strong and consistent material, and songs that were accessible to radio while oozing the spirit of live performance. I spent many hours and days with guitar in hand, playing along to the album and really immersing myself in its sonic splendour.

The album's opening track, 'The Only One', was a made-for-radio rocker with a one-two punch, which contains a super sweet chorus, underscored by a musical simplicity at its core, yet it alludes to sophisticated harmony. It's genius. And for the first time, it also showcases Adams lead guitar playing, the first of two lead guitar solos he does on this album. 'The Only One' is the appropriate offspring to 'Lonely Nights', the opening track on the previous album. I also gave a nod to the track's name — and again proudly wearing my influences on my sleeve — by naming my own song 'Only One' which I released as a single in 2020.

The second track, 'Take Me Back', is a slow-burning groover that builds to a sing-a-long gang vocal refrain and again sees Adams taking the guitar solo. 'Take Me Back' sinks its teeth into you, holding you there for the duration of the tune. The flourishing keyboards, and interplay between rhythm and lead guitar, provide sonic colour to the arrangement. When I first listened to this track on a stereo headphone set, it provided me with a valuable lesson in the importance of the guitars positioning in a song's arrangement and in a stereo mix. Interestingly, the song became a set-list staple during Adams' live performances during the 1980s and one where audience participation became part of the song's live routine.

Next up is 'This Time', a pop-rocker with some very cool textured arpeggio guitar parts during the verses, underscored by a driving solid beat, and topped by a saccharine chorus. I loved the nice ascending melodic line in the bridge too, which ups the ante before the final chorus takes hold.

Track four is 'Straight from the Heart', which was written by an 18-year-old Adams, and was first recorded and released by American singer Ian Lloyd as a single in 1980, as well as, appeared on his album *3WC (Third Wave Civilization)* from the same year. English-born Australian rocker Jon English also recorded and released a much rockier version of the track as a single in 1981 which appears on his *In Roads* album. Here, Adams performs the ballad in a piano-driven setting, that's filled with so much emotive sentiment, you'll need to have a boxes of tissues at the ready.

Side one closes with the title track, 'Cuts Like a Knife' a bona-fide anthemic rocker. The guitars — of course being a guitarist, it's the one instrument I will also notice first and study intently on any piece of music — cut through (pun intended) like a knife amidst the song's mix, and those "na na nas" sing-a-long refrains stick to you like glue, driving the mid-tempo rocker home and Keith Scott's fiery guitar solos are mind-blowing.

The flip-side opens with 'I'm Ready', a scorcher of a rocker, that's best enjoyed with the volume set on 10. Again, the gang vocals rule and along with the guitar power chords, the energy in this song is enough to fuel a jet engine take-off. Adams would later re-record it for his unplugged album, bringing a whole new dimension to the song, without losing any of its inherent power. The next track, 'What's It Gonna Be?' is a masterful piece of power pop that weaves its magic on you. It is also another prime example of the Adams-Vallance song-writing craft. Not only are they master songsmiths, but they also know how to write perfect earworms. Simple yet effective melody lines that grab your attention instantly upon first listening, and then never leave you on repeated listens.

From power-pop we move to the heavy guitar rock of 'Don't Leave Me Lonely'. With chords that smash it out left, right and centre, it's as if The Kinks crashed into KISS and this was the end result. The phasing effect in the drum bridge section is pure gold. It is a track that any guitarist can jam to for hours, just like I used to do in my early years of playing the guitar.

The tempo slows for 'Let Him Know', a throwback to the 1960s wall of sound devised by Phil Spector for his girl groups, but cleverly done here from the male perspective with Adams pleading his heart out. Finally, the album ends with the ballad 'The Best Was Yet to Come', a lighter-waving anthem, that is also a poignant tribute to murdered Playboy Playmate Dorothy

Stratton that also features a rare appearance of Jim Vallance who contributes some very soulful and tasteful electric piano.

I later found out that *Cuts Like a Knife* was Adams' third album, so I began a search for his first two — 1980's eponymous debut and 1981's *You Want It You Got It* — only to be informed they had never been released in Australia and the only way I could get my hands on them were via import. I eventually secured both records and thus began my lifelong love affair with Bryan Adams' music.

At this time I was a couple of years into playing the guitar, and had made great progress. I'd learned all the rudiments of the instrument and, having mastered several songs, I was now beginning to explore sounds and textures. One of the songs on *You Want It You Got It* was called 'Tonight'. The textured guitar sound on that track — the 'new wav-ish' metallic sounding guitar chord splashes, that stamp an anthemic touch to the song — inspired me to seek out some new pedals. At that point I had an overdrive pedal and nothing more. But after hearing this song, I went out and got myself my very first Chorus pedal, which I recall was an Ibanez Stereo Chorus pedal.

At that point in Australia, Adams was an up-and-coming star, but that would change about 18 months later upon the release of his next album *Reckless*, which would turn him into one of the biggest rock and roll artists on the planet, forever imprinting him into the annals of music history. Today, I have every album and recording that was put out by Adams and every other musical project he has been involved in.

Adams' life was changed forever in January 1978 when he met fellow Canadian songwriter and drummer Jim Vallance, who was seven years his senior, and with whom he'd go on to forge a successful song-writing partnership. At that point Vallance had swapped a life of recording and touring as a member of rock band Prism, for a life behind the scenes as a songwriter.

"Prism's first single, 'Spaceship Superstar', did quite well on the Canadian charts, and it got a bit of buzz in the US as well," recalls Vallance, "we hit the road, opening for Heart and Foreigner. Things looked promising, assuming your idea of promising is five guys in a rental car, sleeping in cheap motels and eating microwaved burritos from gas station kiosks on the freeway. Not my idea of a good time! To make matters worse, as we started work on our follow-up album, deep differences emerged. In particular, there was a conflict between me, as the main songwriter, and the guitarist. I wanted to rehearse, to ensure we were as tight a unit as possible. He wanted to jam and keep things loose and lazy. One day during rehearsal things got heated. He swung his guitar at me, narrowly missing my head. That was it. I was out of there.

"I met Bryan not long after I'd quit Prism. We ran into each other by chance at Long and McQuade, a Vancouver guitar store. We exchanged numbers and got together a few days later. That was the beginning of a long creative relationship, although it took five years before we had anything you could call success which would come via 1983's *Cuts Like a Knife* album."

In that same year, the eighteen-year-old Adams would also ink a recording deal with A & M Records for a reputed sum of $1. For Adams it was not about the money, but more about getting that all important first foot in the door. The first fruits of the Adams-Vallance partnership would surface on Adams' self-titled debut album which was issued in early 1980. The debut outing hinted at what would later become his trademark harder-edged, raspy singing style and musically and song-writing wise, showcased what was to come. By the time of his second album, *You Want It You Got It*, released in July 1981, things moved up a further notch, and solidified Adams' sound and image, with the album laying the groundwork for a breakthrough in America. Adams had originally proposed that the album should be titled *Bryan Adams Hasn't Heard of You Either*, which he felt summed up perfectly the nonchalant response the media had given him to his debut release. But it was overruled by the powers that be at his record label. So, they went with *You Want It You Got It* instead as it was less controversial.

In the meantime Adams had continued to tour relentlessly, and this take no prisoners work ethic would continue to hold him in good stead for his entire career. Every success that came Adams' way was hard earned. "I'd been in rehearsals and touring a lot of those songs for a year before hand," Adams told me, "I had worked out my arrangements and sort of had a good vision of how I wanted it to be structurally. So, when I brought these songs to the band in the studio, we worked them up pretty quickly and we banged them out really quickly because we didn't have much time."

With the album done and dusted, he assembled a new line-up for the road. Enter guitarist Keith Scott who would go on to become a staple of Adams' band and with whom, he still remains with today.

"Keith is such a nice fellow and such a good guitar player," says Adams. "When I first met Keith I was 16 and he was already a rock god then. Anybody that had Keith in their band would have all the girls coming to the show. So, he was in demand in that sort of scene back then. And when I first met him, we met on the street, and went for a cup of coffee. We didn't meet in the club, we just bumped into each other in Toronto. I said, 'hey man, you want to go for coffee?' He was like, 'yeah'. And then a few years later, when, after *You Want It, You Got It* was done, I went to him and said, 'Hey, I've just done this record. I'm going to put a band together and go on tour. Do you want to do it?' And he said, 'yeah, maybe'. And I told him that I'd worked with Ric Parnell who was the drummer from Atomic Rooster, in some of my early rehearsals and that really caught Keith's ear. He was like, 'really? Oh, that's interesting'. So, I think that the fact that I was working with musicians that he really respected, helped sort of pave the way for our now very, very long relationship together."

Scott fondly recalled his first time on the road with Adams. "My very first tour with Bryan was eight of us in a rather large van that travelled from city to city in Canada starting in Vancouver heading eastwards," he says. "Of course, some of the distances were rather great and a lot of sleep was lost, it lasted for a few months at least. It wasn't until the following years that the management allowed for an actual tour bus for us. You could sleep in a bed in the bus between gigs! I think this was a great revelation for me and signalled perhaps that there was a possible future for me as a touring musician!"

Scott was enthralled by Adams' work ethic. "In those leaner times upon the release of Bryan's second solo effort, *You Want It, You Got It* and the subsequent tour for it, I witnessed in part how challenging getting one's music played on traditional radio stations of the time were. Bryan didn't let this be an obstacle. Since we roomed together in the first years while touring clubs, I would wake up some mornings, to hear him on the telephone calling radio station managers or programmers at the town we were in, or ones upcoming on our journey, asking them if they were playing his songs and if not, why?

"If that didn't convince them, he'd pay a visit to their station office and try to talk them into it. That is truly door-to-door sales strategy, and in part, a notion of what kind of resolve it takes to start a career in the pop music biz. In fact, he still uses the same personal approach to any new recorded music he releases to this day, nearly 50 years later."

Adams and Vallance continued refining their song-writing craft, while Adams spent the first half of 1982 on the road, his musicianship had grown exponentially. He entered the studio in August 1982 to begin tracking *Cuts Like a Knife*, his third album. Released in January 1983, the album would climb all the way to No.8 on both the US Billboard chart and in Canada, finally delivering Adams a quantum leap into the commercial mainstream. In the US, three singles were officially released off the album: 'Straight from The Heart', the title track and 'This Time'. In Canada and Netherlands though, a fourth single was issued, 'The Best Was Yet to Come'. Adams embarked on an extensive tour in support of *Cuts Like a Knife*, that would keep him on the road for nine straight months, taking in shows in North America, Europe and Japan.

At the start of 1984, as writing sessions for *Reckless* were underway, Adams secured his first Australian tour dates in March 1984 as support for The Police who were in their final leg of their *Synchronicity* tour (which would be The Police's last tour before splitting, though they would reunite for a 2007-08 world tour). The Australian dates saw Vallance filling in on drums for the dates.

"Our routine didn't change much over the years," explains Vallance on how he and Adams approached their song-writing sessions for *Reckless.* "We'd get together every day, seven days a week. Bryan would arrive at my house around noon. We'd have a sandwich and a cup of tea, then we'd play a game of backgammon. Around one o'clock we'd head downstairs to my studio. We might continue working on something we'd started the day before, or we'd pick up our guitars and jam randomly until the beginnings of a new song emerged, then we'd work on that for a while.

"We'd take a dinner break around 7pm. There were a number of restaurants not far from my house. La Cucina (now closed) was one of our regulars. We'd have a nice dinner and a few laughs with Tiberia, the owner, then we'd head back to my studio and work until midnight. The next day we'd start again, and the day after that. Weeks and months the same routine, until we had an album's worth of material. We weren't just writing for Bryan. We also found time to write songs for Bonnie Raitt, Tina Turner, KISS, and many others."

Reckless would turn Adams into a worldwide superstar, forever securing his position among the greats. The song-writing craft that he and Vallance had spent years refining was finally rewarded with Adams' biggest commercial success of his career so far.

"All I can think of when I think of that record is how obsessed I was in making it," Adams told me decades later, "I didn't care how many times we had to re-record it, or re-write it, I just wanted it to be a great listen from start to finish. I remember waking up on the sofa in the control room one day in New York City and everybody had left the studio. We were sharing the studio with another act that was recording in the day time and the session was about to get set up and all I could think was, it's eight in the morning and I wanted to keep recording, but where the hell is everybody? They thought I'd lost it. I mean I made dear Bob Clearmountain (co-producer and engineer) re-mix stuff to the point where he'd got so angry with me and started yelling that I was fucked!"

Yet Adams' obsessive dedication and hard work paid off, he turned 25 on the day that *Reckless* was released [November 5, 1984] and the album would go on to shift more than 12 million in sales internationally, and the heavy touring he undertook in the states resulted in 5 million of US sales alone. The album would also go on to top the US and Canadian album charts, while in Australia it peaked at No.2 — *Reckless* never left my turntable during 1985. While there were several other artists' new albums of that year which were a constant on my playlist, such as John Cougar Mellencamp's *Scarecrow,* Billy Squier's *Signs of Life* and Bruce Springsteen's *Born in The U.S.A.,* not a single day went by for me without a spin of something off *Reckless.* Even today, when I look back over that year, all my memories are sound-tracked by something I played off *Reckless.*

The moment the opening power chords of 'One Night Love Affair' kicks off the album, it sinks their hooks into you and holds you there until the very last note of the album's closer 'Ain't Gonna Cry'. During the summer of 1985, that album could be heard blaring out of my car stereo, and I wore out multiple copies of my cassette too. The album had everything, from pop-rockers such as 'One Night Love Affair' to a power ballad ('Heaven') to heavy guitar rock ('Kids Wanna Rock') to anthems ('Summer of '69') and all points in-between. 'Summer Of '69' also featured a fine example of a key change to create surprise and contrast, providing me with another valuable song-writing lesson in modulation — the changing of a key into another key within the framework of the song structure. In this case, 'Summer Of '69's main key is D major, whilst in the bridge it modulates to a minor third up to F major before returning to its main key at the end.

The album's lead single, 'Run To You' inspired me enormously when I came to later write my own song, 'Fallen Angel' (originally released in 2012 off my album, *Creature of Habit*) where I took the now classic opening arpeggiated guitar riff that lays the foundation to the song, and reversed it, changed key, added a sprinkling of my own notes which led me to carefully construct the opening guitar riff to my song. According to Vallance, 'Run To You' was itself inspired by the main guitar motif to Blue Öyster Cult's '(Don't Fear) The Reaper'. Ironically, the song was first written with the intention to have Blue Öyster Cult record it, but the group turned it down. As Vallance commented, "maybe there wasn't enough cowbell?"

As 1985 began Adams undertook an extensive worldwide tour in support of *Reckless*, which would see him remain on the road for the rest of the year. In between tour dates, Adams still managed to find time to take part in a one-off Canadian supergroup, Northern Lights, that recorded a single 'Tears Are Not Enough' for the sole purpose of raising funds for the devastating famine that was occurring in Ethiopia. As well as contributing guitar to Roger Daltrey's solo album *Under a Raging Moon* which also included two Adams-Vallance co-writes, as well as recording backing vocals to Canadian group Glass Tiger's hit single, 'Don't Forget Me (When I'm Gone)'. In the weeks leading up to Christmas that year, he also issued the appropriately themed, 'Christmas Time' b/w 'Reggae Christmas' single.

Once 1986 came around, thoughts turned to writing and recording a follow-up. But what happens when you have an album that is as hugely successful as *Reckless*? Trying to write a follow-up that will build upon that momentum in order to outsell and overtake the commercial success of its predecessor becomes a huge stumbling block. The pressure is intense.

One example of this particular problem is AC/DC and

their 1980 *Back in Black* album. The follow-up album *For Those About to Rock (We Salute You)* (1981) sold a fraction of what its predecessor sold and the band have never been able to top it since. Nor will they ever. Adams would suffer the same fate commercially with his next album, *Into the Fire* (1987). In my opinion, *Into the Fire* is a brilliant, more introspective, solid outing. The change in subject matter was interesting, and showed another side to the Adams/Vallance song-writing. But the pressure to continue the upward commercial trajectory started to fray the relationship.

"Coming off the huge success of *Reckless* we knew we had big shoes to fill," Vallance confirms, "rather than try and do something bigger, we decided to do something different. Bryan had spent the summer touring with Sting, U2 and Peter Gabriel, doing charity concerts for African famine relief. He was inspired by their cutting-edge sounds and thoughtful lyrics. As a result, we decided to go down that road, or at least give it a try. I purchased an Emulator, a DX-7 and a Prophet 5, digital keyboards that informed and inspired much of the writing we did for the next year.

"Looking back, *Reckless* has a timeless sound to it: real instruments, nothing digital. Conversely, to my ear, *Into the Fire* is of-a-time, sonically stuck in 1987. And for that, I regret the use of those instruments and those sounds. We also steered clear of our previous subject matter — girls, boys and relationships — and we ventured into deeper lyrical territory. For example, we wrote a song about the historic injustices inflicted on native Americans ('Native Son'); and another song about the horrors of the First World War ('Remembrance Day'); and one about a small-town boy with big dreams ('Rebel'); and so on. We made room for a couple of relationship songs, like 'Victim of Love' and 'Hearts on Fire', but even they had a brittle sound, a result of the aforementioned keyboards."

One of the gems on *Into the Fire* is 'Native Son' which closes side one of the album. This six-minute opus begins with a bell-like sounding guitar ringing in a moody and evocative arpeggio riff that sets the atmosphere for the duration of the song. The dynamics build as it twists and turns its way throughout, aptly complimenting the song's poignant subject matter of detailing the mistreatment of the native American community by the white European settlers from the perspective of a native American chief. It also features one of the most underrated guitar solos of all time played by one of the most underrated guitarists of all time, which kicks in around the 4.15-minute mark of the song. It is here where Scott shines in all his resplendent six-string glory. It's one hell of a melodic solo, a story in itself really, an instrumental tune on its own and very much Mark Knopfler inspired, further emphasized by Scott's use of a 1962 Fender Stratocaster. When guitar magazines list their best solos of all time they always seem to include the usual suspects. For example, Jimmy Page's solo on Led Zeppelin's 'Stairway to Heaven', or Slash's on Guns & Roses 'Sweet Child 'O' Mine' or Brian May's on 'Bohemian Rhapsody'. And though each of those are deserving of that title, in my opinion Scott's on 'Native Son' is always overlooked and never gets a mention. I firmly believe that it deserves to be on those lists. Even someone who may not be a guitar player would agree with me, it is highly emotive and soulful, and his clever use of moving from the song's A major key tonality to its more sombre relative F# minor key, further drives home the song's sentiment.

Scott shows his mastery of guitar by restraint, playing just the right amount of notes, never overplaying or underplaying, and his ability to play a solo that is both melodic in structure while not overpowering, is also noteworthy. Sometimes the most understated guitar solos are the most memorable and effective. I've never been a fan of playing a million notes per minute, to me that seems like more of a competitive sport, and at times these solos come across as an ego trip for the player. "Look at me, I can play faster than you and more notes that you!" and while my statement is in no way a slur on this type of playing or player, I have huge respect for it as the technical ability required to play this type of 'shredding' guitar is demanding, this type of playing style is not for me. Give me a solo that one can sing or hum, one that has a melody, one that expresses emotion, feel, soul, and class, any time over a supersonic flurry of notes.

Scott has those qualities of emotional content, feel, tasteful choice of notes, dynamics, when to play and when not to play. He is a truly unsung guitar hero of the past forty years in my honest opinion. And clocking in at almost two minutes, the solo is pure six string bliss. A solo that just keeps on giving no matter how many times you hear it.

****

In the aftermath of the colossal commercial success achieved by *Reckless*, both Adams and Vallance were facing mounting pressures to replicate the album's success when they came to work on *Into the Fire*. Vallance recalls one incident during the recording sessions that illustrates the toll the pressure was taking on all involved. "One day at the studio, when Bob Clearmountain was mixing the title track, I chimed in with a small suggestion. I said, 'Bob, do you think the rhythm guitars could be a bit brighter, like they are on the demo?'. Bob pushed his chair back from the recording console and huffed, 'I don't want *some guy* coming in here and telling me how to get sounds!' I was shocked. I quickly collected myself and said, 'Bob, I'm not *some guy*. I wrote the song'. Which, of course, he knew. Everyone calmed down and the vibe lightened. Bob apologized, but that's one of the moments I remember when I think of that album. It wasn't always pleasant.

"One of my favourite songs is 'Strawberry Fields Forever'. I clearly remember the first time I heard it, on a sunny day in February 1967. I was 14, and what came through the little speaker on my portable turntable was magical. Nearly 60 years later that song still sounds amazing! John Lennon was once asked, what do you remember when you hear 'Strawberry Fields Forever'? And he said, 'I just think of the recording session'. That's how I feel about Bryan's *Into the Fire* album. I just think of the sessions, writing and recording. The memories are a mixed bag, some pleasant, some not so much."

The *Into the Fire* world tour wrapped up in July 1988 and, following a break, Adams also found time to record some backing vocals on 'Sticky Sweet', a track on Mötley Crüe's *Dr. Feelgood* (1989) album, as well as providing backing vocals to the Belinda Carlisle track 'Whatever It Takes' from her *Runaway Horses* (1989) album. The lacklustre performance of *Into the Fire* and its failure to duplicate the commercial success of *Reckless* led to the underlying tensions that had surfaced during the recording sessions coming to a head and the Adams/Vallance partnership split in 1989. It would be another fourteen years before they would resume their song-writing partnership.

"Beginning in August 1988, Bryan and I met daily, with a view to assembling a follow-up to *Into the Fire*, an album that hadn't performed anywhere near as well as *Reckless*," Vallance explains. "To be honest, it was a chore. Most days our writing seemed forced, without direction or focus. Even worse, we weren't enjoying one another's company. By this point we'd spent more than ten years writing songs together, much of it in a small room with no windows. If that's not a recipe for getting on one another's nerves, I don't know what is. We needed to take a break from one another, but we didn't. We kept working. Eventually, predictably, things came to a boil. One day I rang Bryan and announced that I was done. I had nothing more to contribute and I walked away. Mutt helped finish what Bryan and I had started, and to both their credits, the results were outstanding."

Having now split from Vallance, Adams hooked up with U2 producer Steve Lillywhite and began initial recording sessions with him, but the outcome wasn't to Adams' satisfaction so Lillywhite was removed from the project and Bob Clearmountain returned as producer in 1989 and the tracks re-recorded but again, the end result was not up to par with Adams, so a third attempt was made, this time with Mike Fraser who had been assistant engineer on *Cuts Like a Knife* and

Reckless. That too proved unsuccessful. The deadlock was only broken when Adams teamed up with uber-producer Robert "Mutt' Lange, the man behind mega-selling albums by Def Leppard, AC/DC and Foreigner.

According to Adams, working with Lange was a case of "learning as you go" he told me. It likened it to "sort of going through the university of rock. Jim and I would spend a year writing a record and then recording it and Mutt and I did the same thing too. So, *Waking Up the Neighbours* took a year and a half to make because we were writing as we were going, and sometimes we'd get to the point where a song was, 'yeah, that's feeling pretty good, except that bit doesn't work, so let's change it', and then we'd muck around with that for a bit. And he got the best performances out of me, out of my voice that anyone's ever got."

Released in September 1991, *Waking Up the Neighbours* would return Adams to the commercial heights of *Reckless*, with the album topping the charts in countless countries around the world. The lead single issued from the album, '(Everything I Do) I Do It for You' would feature in the film, *Robin Hood: Prince of Thieves* and go on to garner Adams the longest stay at No.1 in the UK where it clocked up a record sixteen consecutive weeks. The song also spent seven weeks at the top of the US Billboard chart.

'Everything I Do (I Do It For You)' saw the pair of Mutt Lange and Adams joined by American film composer and orchestral arranger Michael Kamen whose initial melody inspired the song. Kamen would later repeat the process offering up initial melodies to Lange and Adams for both 'All for Love' and 'Have You Ever Really Loved a Woman?' all of which delivered Adams number one hits.

A month after the album, Adams embarked on the *Waking Up the World* tour, one of his most extensive world tours in support of the album. He would finally make his way to Australia for his first headlining shows in February 1992 as part of the world tour, which itself would run until December

1993. Towards the tail end of the tour, a compilation album of some of Adams biggest and best songs up to that point was assembled and issued in November 1993 as *So Far So Good*. The album featured an unreleased song, 'Please Forgive Me' which was released as a single. The trio of albums — *So Far So Good*, *Waking Up the Neighbours* and *Reckless* — have gone on to become Adams' three biggest selling albums in his catalogue. 'All for Love' which saw Adams team up with Rod Stewart and Sting, would be the soundtrack of the 1993 film, *The Three Musketeers*. Soon after the completion of the tour, Adams began the *So Far So Good* tour which saw Adams return to Australia in January/February 1994. Adams boom with chart-topping film songs would extend into 1995 when 'Have You Ever Really Loved a Woman?' was used in the film *Don Juan DeMarco*.

It wouldn't be until 1996 before Adams' next studio album would appear. Titled, *18 til I Die* he again teamed up with *Waking Up the Neighbours* producer "Mutt" Lange, the album was another commercial hit, continuing Adams' winning streak.

"It was interesting times for us then around 1995-96 as the music genres were shifting," recalls Scott. "Nirvana had released *Nevermind* around the same time as *Wakin Up the Neighbours* came out, so popular tastes were changing. I think Mutt and Bryan might have tried to capture some of that spirit while they were writing the album. And prior to that Mutt's energy had shifted slightly to begin his new venture with Shania Twain. The rest is history. I think at the time, *18 til I Die* could have used a bit more time and a few more songs to be part of it all, but there was pressure from all sides to get a record out.

"Again, Mutt was really great to be involved with, and he actually played most of the guitar on the track *18 til I Die* along with Bryan. I remember leaving the session and they wrote a few more songs and played the parts themselves. And there were a few guests too, such as flamenco guitarist Paco de Lucia [on 'Have You Ever Really Loved a Woman?'] and Phil Palmer a session guitarist from England who played on 'I'll Always Be Right There'. And a lot of my overdubbed guitars were done in Jamaica and France during 1995."

Session guitarist Phil Palmer remembers his recording session for 'I'll Always Be Right There' as being "very relaxed". "I was living in Antibes in the south of France at the time, Bryan and Mutt had rented a villa up the coast in St Tropez with a mobile studio set up. I received a call from Michael Kamen who was a very close chum and he suggested I throw an acoustic guitar in the car and drive down. They [Bryan and Mutt] had an idea of what they wanted me to play and I was able to get close, though I'm sure that some editing was done after the event."

Noodling around on the guitar one day during one of the sessions for *18 till I Die* would later reap Scott an unexpected credit on a Britney Spears track, 'Don't Let Me Be the Last to Know' that appears on her chart-topping album, *Oops!... I Did It Again*. "There was a moment during the recording for *18 til I Die* where I was on a break to edit," explains Scott, "I was playing a certain chord sequence to occupy myself when Mutt suddenly asked me what it was and I said that it was just something I was working on. Then a couple years later, he contacted me and notified me that he had used the chord sequence for one on 'Don't Let Me Be the Last to Know' and that he wanted to credit me. He had remembered what it [the chord sequence] was!"

In September 1997 Adams performed for MTV's Unplugged series of concerts, which showcased acts reworking their material in a non-electrified format. The concert would be recorded and issued just in time for Christmas of that year, simply as *Bryan Adams — Unplugged* and would also feature three new songs; the up-tempo and highly infectious 'Back to You' which would be released as a single, 'When You Love Someone', and 'A Little Love'.

On a Day Like Today, Adams' eighth studio outing, followed in 1998 and featured Adams duetting with Spice Girl Melanie C on one of the album's singles, 'When You're Gone'. A track titled 'Cloud Number Nine' was remixed by English electronic artist Chicane and released as a single too. Adams and Chicane would later collaborate again with Adams co-writing and providing vocals to 'Don't Give Up' which would be issued as a single from Chicane's 2000 album *Behind the Sun.*

After a one-off radio appearance sparked the idea, Adams decided to change tack and go out as a three piece between 1998 to 2002. It saw Adams switch from guitar to playing bass, with Keith Scott handling both rhythm and lead guitar parts and Mickey Curry on drums, and with all three clothed in matching white attire. In several media interviews at the time Adams described the three-piece experience as one of the best in his life.

"That [three-piece] idea was hatched by Bryan as a stopgap until he had a much clearer idea of a path to take," recalls Scott. "I initially felt that it might be a year, maybe two at most. Alas, almost five years later, we were obliged to add keys as a result of the *Spirit* soundtrack which we were going to promote, so from there it gradually went back to the standard five piece again. Actually six, since we used a percussionist for a while too."

Did Scott find performing double duties of both lead and rhythm guitar playing, a daunting prospect? "It was a challenge to cover so many parts on just electric guitar but there were some nice moments along the way. I feel Bryan's music deserves the most instrumentation as possible since the arrangements originally had the most to offer. But it was a cool way to express it in the three-piece setting."

Spirit: Stallion of the Cimarron which appeared in 2002, was the soundtrack Adams had composed to the animated film of the same name, with the track 'Here I Am' issued from the album as Adams' next official single. Now back in full band mode, Adams embarked on the *Here I Am* tour, that same year. When it came to Adams' next studio album, 2004's *Room Service*, he took a completely different approach yet again when it came to the recording process. Rather than entering a recording studio, all the material on the album was recorded while Adams was on tour in Europe, utilizing a compact suitcase of recording gear which he set up in various hotel rooms and backstage areas during the many hours of downtime between shows, hence the title.

I caught several Bryan Adams concerts in Australia over the years, some of the memories of the earlier concerts are a bit hazy today, but some of the later ones I caught remain fresh in my mind. I recall his Rod Laver Arena show in March 2005 as part of the Australian tour in support of the *Room Service* album. This is what I remember from that show.

> As the clock struck 9 pm and the lights dimmed, the loud roar of the audience reverberated throughout the arena as Adams and his band hit the stage. What followed was a greatest hits-laden set that was occasionally contrasted with some material off the new album. It was a show that oozed infectious energy and a party vibe. And as it had become a regular feature by then, during 'When You're Gone' he offered one lucky female audience member to join him on stage to duet on the track. It proved to be a hilarious moment, bringing much good, spirited laughter all round. Adams certainly made it a night to remember, with an encore that saw him in acoustic solo mode for several songs.

Having enjoyed the process for *Room Service,* and with Adams still adhering to a busy touring schedule, he repeated the recording process for many of the tracks that appeared on his next album, 2008's *11*. It also saw Adams reunite with former song-writing partner Jim Vallance for three of the album tracks. They had begun to rekindle their relationship around the time of *Room Service.* Two years later Adams took another left turn, embarking on his *Bare Bones* tour. It saw Adams on acoustic guitar accompanied by pianist Gary Breit take to the road in a series of intimate, stripped-back performances. A selection of some of the best live performances recorded in the early months of the *Bare Bones* tour, were collected and released in late 2010 as a live album entitled, *Bare Bones.*

When the tour finally hit Australia in September 2011, I was there again, with a front row seat at the Palais Theatre to watch him perform one of the most memorable and intimate concerts I've ever seen, and hearing all the hits in their unadorned beauty, was truly magical. A covers album, *Tracks of My Years,* followed in 2014 that showcased Adams paying tribute to some of his favourite songs and aside from his choice re-imaginings, one original song 'She Knows Me' from the Adams-Vallance pen was also included. While working on the covers album, Adams also busied himself with another album, working with ELO's Jeff Lynne who helmed production on his next album 2015's *Get Up* which highlighted a more straightforward retro vibe that paid homage to Adams' early rock and roll roots, all filtered through the very Jeff Lynne signature sounding production sheen. Around the same time, Adams and Vallance ventured into new waters, writing material for the stage musical production of *Pretty Woman*, which was based on the 1990 film. The musical would make its debut on Broadway in 2018.

"We were hired in November 2015 as a result of a positive and productive meeting at the New York apartment of director Jerry Mitchell," Vallance recalls, "producer Paula Wagner and screen-writer JF Lawton were also present at the meeting. Bryan and I started working on songs right away. In January 2016 we met again with Jerry and the others in Chicago, where it was -40c outside! Perfect weather for staying indoors and getting lots of work done! Writing continued in London, Canada, and wherever Bryan and I were able to meet, in and around his tour schedule. We also made progress online, sending audio files back and forth by email."

Eventually the pair ended up with forty songs in total, with sixteen making the final cut for the musical, and three ending up being re-recorded for later Adams albums; 'Please Stay' (on *Ultimate*), 'I Could Get Used to This' (on *Shine a Light*) and 'I've Been Looking for You' (on *So Happy It Hurts*). The remaining songs were rejected, and never saw the light of day. Compared to their usual modus operandi in writing material for artists and albums, working on the musical proved to be different. "The director would provide instructions, and we'd go away and write a song, and present it to him," explains Vallance on the writing process. "He might like it for a day or two — or sometimes a week or two — then he'd toss it out and ask for something different. It was a painful process. A carpenter friend once told me, I can build you a beautiful shelf for your books but if you ask me to rip it out and build it again, I won't do quite as good a job the second time. If you ask me to rip it out a third time, I'll build it again, but you won't get anything close to my best effort. That's what it was like working on a musical, or at least that's what it's like working with a difficult, demanding director. The first year of writing was quite enjoyable but the second and third year of re-writing and re-re-writing was immensely frustrating. I nearly quit on more than one occasion. Bryan had to talk me off the ledge."

In 2017 another compilation, *Ultimate*, was released. It was a 21-song set of some of his best and most well-loved material including two new songs; 'Ultimate Love' and the *Pretty Woman* left-over, 'Please Stay'. As the decade came to a close, 2019 saw *Shine a Light*, Adams' fourteenth studio outing, issued and as has been Adams' modus operandi since day one, he continued touring, this time embarking on the *Shine A Light* Tour in support of the new disc. As the tour rolled over into and through 2020, it came to a sudden halt, as did everything else in the world, when the global pandemic hit. Not one to sit around, Adams continued working on new music and other projects from within the confines of his recording studio.

Post-pandemic, he resumed the tour and released *So Happy It Hurts* in 2022 which Adams had worked on during the lockdowns of the pandemic. The album saw him playing most of the instruments, with contributions by his band members recorded remotely. Having endured the gloom of the past two years, the album provided the perfect antidote to the times, with its uplifting and feel-good spirit.

May 2022 saw Adams headline a three-night residency at London's famed Royal Albert Hall. The shows, which were originally scheduled for May 2020 but postponed due to the pandemic, saw Adams perform three of his classic albums in their entirety, with one album showcased each night. Beginning with *Cuts Like a Knife* on night one, *Into the Fire* on night two and *Waking up The Neighbours* on the third and final night. The shows were recorded and later released in December 2023 as *Live at The Royal Albert Hall.*

2022 also saw Adams re-recording and reworking a collection of his hits and issuing them via two albums; *Classic* and *Classic Pt II* in 2022. Continuing his busy schedule into 2023, he released the soundtrack to the *Pretty Woman — The Musical* and contributed two new songs; 'You're Awesome' and 'Sometimes You Lose Before You Win', to the soundtrack to the television film, *Office Race.*

Having clocked up more than forty-five years in the business, Adams has managed to navigate his way successfully through the exploitive world of the music industry, unlike some who have succumbed to the darker elements of the industry and fallen by the wayside. For Adams, his utmost devotion to his musical craft, boundless energy, steadfast work ethic and business acumen has held him in good stead.

"I was never interested in getting wasted, and I can't imagine how much I'd have been ripped off by the music business if I hadn't had my wits about me," Adams told me in October 2023 in an exclusive interview for my 'Musical Musings' music column in the *Shepparton News*. "But even though I did, I got horribly robbed by people in the business. I was young, naïve and excited… I was the perfect target."

Afterword

Looking back over my musical life I became acutely aware that the years from around the middle of the 1970s to the early part of the 1980s strongly dominated, laying the foundation of the music that would play a huge role in my musical journey. The artists from that era, from ABBA to Gerry Rafferty, and from Bryan Adams to Billy Squier, all initially sprang from that time period. And when I listen to my own music today, I keep noticing those influences seeping through. Somehow, that period in music history for me, transcends all time and space and has been pivotal.

Nostalgia is a wonderful thing. One's life is comprised of experiences of the past which is always shaping who you are and what is possible in the future. As life moves on though, things change so one can't stand still in the past. It's important to be present and always looking towards the future and, although I'm a child of the seventies, I'm also a man of today. It's interesting to have witnessed some of the newish bands I have written about in this book, those that came up in the early years of the new millennium. Though I had the privilege of having a front row seat to many of them, just observing the trajectory of their careers in this ever-changing music industry, has been both enlightening and revealing.

It seems to me that the music artists of today stand far less chance of staying the distance compared to those from what I consider the golden age of music. There are many reasons for this, some fall into the trappings of fame and fortune, while others, due to the harshness of the business, come to a realization that the enormous sacrifices required to sustain any kind of life-long career in music are not worth it in the long run, especially when it comes to having a steady income stream, which most in the creative arts are ever so aware of.

Then there are the lucky few that are called to it, and are in it for the long haul, knowing all too well that life isn't always going to be easy and that the lowest of lows is nothing more than character building and needs to be accepted as part and parcel of the path chosen. "Whatever doesn't kill you, makes you stronger," as German philosopher Friedrich Nietzsche once stated.

Wearing rose-tinted glasses in this industry, which highly values fantasy over reality, won't do you any good. What will, though, is being true to yourself, and having a mindset that is focused on the realities of what a creative life in music fully entails. At the end of the day, it is what gives you meaning to who you are and your life, and what will safely navigate you through the rollercoaster ride necessary for a life in music.

Acknowledgements

Many thanks to my wife Liz, Ashley Shaw and all at Empire Publications, Mick Middles, Pat Prince at *Goldmine* magazine, Warren Kurtz, and everyone who purchased and enjoyed my first book, *Backstage Pass: The Grit and The Glamour.*

The author wishes to also thank the following artists and individuals for the interviews that were conducted by the author for inclusion in this book: Bryan Adams, Gerry Beckley, Mick Box, Jon Brewer, Ron Burman, Alan Clark, Steve Conte, Mitch Davis, Paul Dean, Paul French, Graham Gouldman, Mark Goodman, Alex Greenwald, Ian Haugland, Justin Hayward, Paul Hirsh, Chris Hook, Philip Israel, Al Jardine, Paul Jones, Marty Jourard, Phil Manzanera, Troy McLawhorn, Larry Mitchell, Declan O'Doherty, Phil Palmer, Jeff Pilson, Graham Preskett Alan Rafferty, Jim Rafferty, Martha Rafferty, Darren Robinson, Janne Schaffer, Keith Scott, Jay Sosnicki, John Steel, Billy Squier, Gary Taylor, Jim Vallance, Adrian Vandenberg, James Warren, Mike Watson and Snowy White.

Printed in Poland
by Amazon Fulfillment
Poland Sp. z o.o., Wrocław

36291716R00131